DO THIS,
NOT THAT

10
CRITICAL
DECISIONS

THAT WILL MAKE
OR BREAK YOUR
REAL ESTATE
INVESTMENT

MICHAEL LANTRIP
Attorney | Accountant | Investor

THE AUTHOR

Michael Lantrip, Attorney at Law, is licensed to practice law in Texas, North Carolina, Virginia, and the District of Columbia.

He has a B.B.A. in Finance from the University of Houston School of Business, and he has a Juris Doctor (J.D.) in Law from the University of Texas School of Law.

He is admitted to practice Law in all Courts in Texas, North Carolina, Virginia, and the District of Columbia, as well as the U.S. Tax Court, the U.S. Federal District Court, Eastern District of Texas, and the D.C. Court of Appeals.

He is a member of the National Society of Accountants.

He practices in the fields of Tax Law, Real Estate Law, Corporate and Business Law, and Wills, Trusts and Estates.

Formerly a Tax Examiner for the IRS, and a Tax Accountant for a Big 8 Accounting Firm, he has also been a Military Intelligence Analyst, Newspaper Reporter, Radio Announcer, Radio News Director, Television Reporter and Anchorman, and Television Executive News Producer.

He has handled over 2,000 criminal cases.

In addition to 40 years of practicing law, he built one of the first Computerized Abstract Plants, and operated his own Title Insurance Company, becoming an Approved Title Attorney for seven national Title Insurance Underwriters.

He has handled over 2,000 real estate closings.

Prior to his law career, he was a Radio Announcer at WQTE in Detroit during the "Motown" era, and he was a DJ at KIKK in Houston when it was named "Country Music Station of the Year" by Billboard Magazine.

He collects and refurbishes Vintage Audio Equipment.

He has written and produced more than 1,000 half-hour Television Newscasts.

He has written over 700 stories as a Newspaper Reporter.

He has logged over 8,000 hours on the radio.

He is a Lifetime Member of Mensa.

As a Real Estate Investor, his activities have ranged from travel trailers to office buildings, and from on-campus condos to rural land.

He was named a Top Writer by Quora.com, where his Answers have been viewed more than 2,630,000 times.

He has written and published 9 books:

1.) "How To Do A Section 1031 Like Kind Exchange"

2.) "OMNIBUS EDITION How To Do A Section 1031 Like Kind Exchange: Real Estate, NNN, DST, and T-I-C"

3.) "50 Real Estate Investing Calculations"

4.) "Tax Cuts And Jobs Act For Real Estate Investors"

5.) "Your Best Business Entity For Real Estate Investing"

6.) "10 Other Real Estate Investments You Could Do"

7.) "Real Estate Investing Vocabulary of Terms"

8.) "Section 121 Real Estate Investing System"

9.) "Do This, Not That!"

All are available in print and digital on Amazon.

His Amazon Author Page is:

www.amazon.com/Michael-Lantrip/e/B01N2ZRGUY

His Quora page is:

www.quora.com/profile/Michael-Lantrip-1

His personal website is MichaelLantrip.com.

COPYRIGHT PAGE

DISCLAIMER

Although I am a lawyer, I am not your lawyer. I would be honored if I were, but I am not.

Reading this book does not create an attorney-client relationship between us. This book should not be used as a substitute for the advice of a competent attorney admitted or authorized to practice law in your jurisdiction.

TABLE OF CONTENTS

INTRODUCTION

Real Estate Investing is not all sunshine and lollipops.

It's a business.

And, like life itself, Real Estate Investing can be tough.

You pay for your mistakes, but you are rewarded for your knowledge, your ability, and for your hard work.

There are actual Rules, not written down but real nonetheless, and they self-enforce.

Sorry to preach, but stick with me, this will help you.

Life is all about making decisions.

Sometimes, it seems like we make our most critical decisions when we are in the worst position to be making decisions.

Now, even though Real Estate Investing decisions are not always life-altering, they are still very important.

Fortunately, we have more time to think about Real Estate Investing decisions, and we have access to more information.

And even if we make the wrong decision, we can still correct it, if we know how.

In this book, we'll be looking at some of the decisions that you might be making, looking at what happens when you get them wrong, or don't pick the best option, and then, step-by-step, how the same situation should have been handled.

These stories are made up, the people are not real, but the facts are real.

And the consequences are definitely real.

This is a very unforgiving business.

But you can use that situation to your advantage.

Usually when you find a great deal, it is because somebody else screwed up.

If you understand the big picture, how everything is connected, and how to move the parts around, you can turn someone else's problem into your opportunity.

And you can avoid being one of those people who screwed up.

Real Estate Investing is all about knowledge, and the more you have, the more successful you will be.

Let's get started.

CHAPTER 1

CASH-OUT OR LEASE/ PURCHASE

OVERVIEW

A Lease/Purchase is a transaction that involves one property, two people, and a written document.

The property is real estate.

The first person is the Owner of the property, referred to here as the Lessor because he is leasing the property that he owns.

The second person is called the Lessee. He is the person who is acquiring a Lease on the property, with the Lease containing terms under which the Lessee will eventually be entitled to purchase the property.

And the written document is called a Lease/ Purchase Agreement.

The person in this first Chapter didn't use one, but perhaps he should have.

Let's look at it both ways.

WHAT HAPPENED

Five years ago, John bought a Duplex for $300,000.

He made a 30% Down Payment of $90,000.

He got a Mortgage for $210,000.

Now it is five years later, and the $300,000 Duplex is worth $400,000.

The $210,000 Mortgage has been paid down to a Remaining Principal Balance of $200,000.

So, John sells the Duplex for $400,000.

His transaction costs are $10,000.

Therefore, his Net Sale Price is $390,000.

This amount is also his Gross Sales Proceeds.

The Remaining Principal Balance of $200,000 on the $210,000 Mortgage is then paid from the Gross Sales Proceeds, leaving $190,000.

This is John's Net Sales Proceeds. That's what he walks away from the Closing table with.

Now, $190,000 is a good number for five years of ownership.

But wait, we need to look more closely at the number, in order to understand what it really means, because it is not his "profit," even though that's what it looks like.

This $190,000 number is actually made up of 3 other numbers, and we need to know what they are so that we can analyze the transaction, and then compare it to an alternative transaction later.

The first number involved in our breakdown is $90,000.

This is how much of his own money that John put into the investment, his Down Payment.

That money is now, in effect, being returned to him. It is part of the check he receives at Closing.

The second number we look at is the $10,000.

This is the amount by which the Mortgage was reduced. He borrowed $210,000 but he paid back $200,000.

The reason for this reduction is that, over time, as he made payments on the Note, those payments, including both Principal and Interest, represented John paying down the amount of Principal due on his Mortgage, with the payments being made from his own personal funds.

Mortgage Payments are comprised of both Principal and Interest. The Interest portion of each payment was deducted by John from his Gross

Rental Income as an Expense on his tax return. But the Principal portion of each payment was not deductible.

So, this $10,000 portion of the $190,000 Net Sales Proceeds is the amount by which the Principal of the Loan was paid down, and is also, in effect, the return of his own money.

This leaves the third number, $90,000.

This is John's before-tax profit on the investment.

It happened because the Fair Market Value of the Duplex when John bought it was $300,000 and that's what John paid.

When John sold it, the Fair Market Value had gone up to $400,000 and that's what John sold it for.

The Gross Profit was $100,000.

John's costs of the transaction was $10,000.

So, John's Net Profit, before taxes, was $90,000.

But to get a real-life picture, we need to go further, and look at the after-tax number, the money that John eventually ended up with, after paying taxes.

His tax liability will be of two types, and of two amounts.

Don't be intimidated by tax numbers, they are easy to understand.

The first tax will be his Depreciation Recapture Tax.

The Depreciation Recapture Tax is the tax equal to 25% of the dollar amount of Depreciation that John claimed on the Duplex for the five years that he owned it. He deducted this amount each year (on his tax return) from the property's Operating Income as an expense, even though it was not an actual cash, out-of-pocket, expense.

John claimed $10,000 each year in Depreciation, for a total of $50,000 in Depreciation over the 5-year period.

Now he is taxed on the Depreciation that he has claimed, at the rate of 25%.

And 25% of $50,000 is $12,500.

So John's Depreciation Recapture Tax is $12,500 and this reduces his before-tax profit from $90,000 to $77,500.

See how easy that was?

The second tax liability that John has will be the Capital Gains Tax.

Capital Gains Tax is an income-type tax levied on his Net Profit of $90,000.

But it is not like your regular income taxes.

Capital Gains are taxed differently from regular income.

And the Capital Gains Tax rate is not the same for everyone.

Taxpayers fall into different tax brackets for Capital Gains taxation, depending on the amount of their total Adjusted Gross Income.

The Capital Gains tax brackets are 0%, 15%, and 20%.

John's income places him in the 15% tax bracket, so his Capital Gains tax is 15% of $90,000 which is $13,500.

This reduces his remaining $77,500 before-tax profit down to $64,000 after-tax profit.

So, let's summarize.

John sold his Duplex after five years of ownership, and he got back his $90,000 down payment, his $10,000 note pay-down, and $64,000 in profit.

That's what happened.

Now, let's look at what probably should have happened, and make a comparison.

WHAT SHOULD HAVE HAPPENED

We have the same set of facts.

Five years ago, John bought a Duplex for $300,000 and it is now worth $400,000.

When he bought it, he paid $90,000 down and got a Mortgage for $210,000. That Mortgage has now been paid down to $200,000.

But here's where he uses a different strategy.

He doesn't just sell the property and cash out.

Now he refinances the existing $200,000 debt on the Duplex to $300,000 at 5% for 25 years, with a monthly payment of $1,750.

John puts the $100,000 in his pocket. It is non-taxable because it is a loan.

It represents, in effect, the return of his $90,000 Down Payment, plus the $10,000 pay-down of the Mortgage.

So he has that back in his pocket, tax-free.

And he still owns the property, which still has $100,000 of equity in it (the difference between the $400,00 Fair Market Value and the $300,000 debt), and the property is still producing monthly rental income.

But now that John has the $100,000 back that he invested in the property, he really wants to rid himself of the day-to-day management responsibilities, and spend time looking at some other investments, while continuing to own the property for the annual appreciation, and for the strength and status that it provides for his Financial Statement.

So he finds a responsible and dependable individual looking for a good real estate deal, and he does a Lease With Option To Purchase.

And it really is "a good real estate deal," so he should have no trouble finding a responsible and dependable individual.

The terms are no money down, 10-year term, $1,800 per month, with the Lessee paying for insurance, repairs, and taxes. And each unit is currently rented for $2,000 per month, and this amount will double over the 10-year period of the lease.

In return, the Lessee also receives 20% of each monthly note payment amount as a "credit toward purchase" of the property.

So, at this point, John has $100,000 of non-taxable cash, he still owns the property which has another $100,000 of equity, and he has no management responsibilities, just as though he had sold the property.

The Lease payments of $1,800 per month on his Lease/Purchase Agreement cover his Note payments of $1,750 per month.

Of course, the $1,800 per month that John is receiving in Lease payments represent Gross Income and the payments are taxable to him as such. But he can deduct from the $1,800 as he receives it, 2/3 of the $1,200 per month in interest that he is paying on his own Note (the portion that represents the refinanced note), and he can also deduct $833 in monthly Depreciation that he is still allowed to claim on the property because he still owns it, for a total of over $2,000 per month.

So he will probably even have a small paper loss in the beginning, before his interest payments start decreasing.

In 10 years, when the Purchase Option is exercised, the Duplex will probably have a Fair Market Value of $765,000 because it has been appreciating in value the historic 6.7% amount annually.

The Lessee will be entitled to a Purchase Credit of $43,200 as the accumulation of the 20% credits for each Lease payment.

After the $43,200 credit to the Lessee, the Sales Price will be $721,800.

After John pays off the $212,000 remaining Principal Balance on his Note, he will be left with $509,800 in cash.

This is his Net Sales Proceeds, and it is also his before-tax profit.

John will have two tax liabilities, the Depreciation Recapture Tax and the Capital Gains Tax.

John claimed $10,000 in Depreciation each year for 15 years, for a total of $150,000.

His Depreciation Recapture Tax of 25% will be $37,500.

His Capital Gains is $721,800 minus $300,000 which is $421,800.

His Capital Gains Tax of 15% will be $63,270.

So, John's total tax liability will be $37,500 plus $63,270 which is $100,770.

After paying this out of the $509,800 Net Sales Proceeds, John is left with $409,030 as his after-tax profit.

Compare this to the $64,000 profit in our first scenario.

But remember, this is 10 years from now.

In order to compare these numbers to the sale that we described above, we need to know how much $409,030 in 10 years is worth in today's dollars. And the answer is that it is about $300,000 in today's dollars, using an Inflation Rate of 3%.

So, in total, for keeping the property, refinancing it, and leasing it with a purchase option, John will receive:

1.) $100,000 cash now, non-taxable,

2.) $409,030 in ten years, which has a Present Value of about $300,000,

3.) The positive benefits derived during that ten years from owning a Duplex with a FMV of over $400,000 and the value going up each year, without the responsibility of management. These benefits include a very impressive Income Statement and Balance Sheet and a very strong Credit Score. The equity will also be there for John to borrow against, if he needs it sooner.

This $509,030 cash with a Present Value of $400,000, plus continued ownership of the property for 10 years, compares with $164,000 received in an outright sale.

CONCLUSION

Using a Lease/Purchase allows John to end up with about two and a half times as much cash as he would receive with an outright sale.

And the risk-free, trouble-free ownership of the Duplex for another ten-year period is an even bigger factor.

After you have become an established Real Estate Investor, you understand the importance of constantly "being in the game."

That means owning as much real estate as you can at a reasonable risk level, generating as much cash flow as you can, and it means holding onto property for as long as you can.

The first house that I bought is now selling for about 20 times what I paid for it.

Damn!

SELECTED RESOURCES

FREE ONLINE AMORTIZATION SCHEDULE

Real Estate Investing is all about Time and Money.

You always need to look at a visual representation of both, whether you are Buying or Selling.

I always start with an Amortization Schedule.

Here is the one that I have found to be the best.

www.MortgageCalculator.org/calcs/amortization.php

CAPITAL GAINS AND DEPRECIATION RECAPTURE EXPLAINED

Capital Gains are pretty easy to understand, but are often discussed with Depreciation included, and the two must be separated in order for Capital Gains to be fully understood.

Here is an older website that I built that still has some very valuable content relating to Section 1031 Exchanges and to Capital Gains and Depreciation Recapture.

Scroll down in the right sidebar to the Categories Section.

www.S1031Exchange.com/capital-gains-tax

TIME VALUE OF MONEY CALCULATION

It is critical that you understand this concept.

You can read about this Calculation, and many other Calculations, in my book, "50 Real Estate Investing Calculations."

amazon.com/dp/B077ZFNZKN

The following Calculation is from Section 47 in the book.

The Time Value of Money just means that money in your hand right now is worth more than the same amount of money that you will receive in the future.

If you have $100,000 and purchase a 12-month Certificate of Deposit that will pay you 1% interest, then a year from now you will have $101,000.

So, $100,000 in your hand right now is worth more than $100,000 that you would receive a year from now, because you can invest the $100,000 that you have right now and turn it into $101,000 a year from now, which is $1,000 more than the $100,000 that you have right now.

This is the Time Value of Money.

It cannot be ignored, it must be part of all of your decisions, and it will be a vital part of most of your Real Estate Investing Calculations.

We can see what the Present Value Calculation looks like.

PV = A ÷ [(1 + R) multiplied by itself "N" times], where

PV is the Present Value,

A is the amount of money we are dealing with,

R is the stated interest rate, and

N is the number of periods we are applying the calculation.

But the easier way to use it is to go to one of the online calculators that I identify in my book.

https://www.calculatorsoup.com/calculators/financial/present-value-calculator-basic.php

This is a very valuable Calculation, and you should be using it often.

Learn how each element relates to the other, and you will discover other ways to use it in your real estate investing.

CHAPTER 2

PRE-(NOT REALLY) APPROVED

OVERVIEW

"Pre-Approved" is a term used by Lenders when they are telling Loan Applicants the status of their Loan Application.

The Loan Applicant believes what he is told, that he is at some sevel of approval, but it is usually just a ploy by the Lender to keep him involved in the application process until the Lender decides whether or not to make the loan.

"Pre-Approved" actually means that the loan <u>has not</u> been approved.

And, in reality, at this point, it also means that there is no reason to believe that it will be approved.

Think about it.

The term "Approved" means that the loan has been approved, obviously.

Everything other than "Approved" does not mean that the loan has been approved.

Therefore, "Pre-Approved" does not mean that the loan has been approved.

You're supposed to think that "Pre-Approved" means that you have been approved ahead of time. But it does not mean that.

If the term "Pre-Approved" means anything, it means that you have provided the Lender with all of the documentation required, and you have not been turned down yet.

The reason that you have not been turned down yet, and the reason that you have not been approved yet, is that the person or committee that will be making the decision on the Loan Application has not even seen your loan application package at this point in the loan application process.

But let's get into the details and see how this common practice might have serious consequences for you.

WHAT HAPPENED

Alice owned a Townhouse in a row of Townhouses that were gradually being bought up and turned into rentals.

Some of the activity in the area was no longer what she was comfortable with, and she was not enjoying her lifestyle as much as she did when she bought the property a few years ago.

She had been thinking of selling, and buying a house closer to her job, but she had not gotten around to actually doing anything about it.

Then one day she received a decent offer from the owner of the adjacent Townhouse, who was a Real Estate Investor who also owns some of the other Townhouses.

Alice thought that she might be interested, so she looked around and was surprised to find the perfect property for her, in a new development, and at a good price.

She went to her Lender and applied for a loan.

She answered all of their questions, and was told that she was "pre-qualified."

Then she provided her W-2s and Tax Returns and bank statements for three years, along with all of the other documentation required, and after more than a month, she was finally told that she had been "pre-approved" for the loan, and that they could fund the loan whenever she was ready.

So she signed the contract to buy the property, put down the $20,000 Earnest Money, and was told that the closing would take place in 30-45 days.

She did not put a clause in the Sales Contract stating that the purchase was contingent on getting financing approval, because the Lender had already told her that she was pre-approved.

She also signed the Contract to sell her Townhouse, and agreed to a Closing Date within 30-45 days, at her option, with a two-week moving-out period after that.

Then the Lender began asking for more documents, which she supplied, and even requesting a larger Down Payment, which she agreed to, because she didn't really have much choice.

The Closing Date was scheduled by the Title Company for a couple of weeks later, and she was relieved.

Then she got an Email from the Title Company a few days before Closing saying that the Lender had still not sent a Funding Number, and also that the Lender would not commit to when they would be providing one.

Alice contacted the Lender, and was told that the new development in which she was buying a home was not yet sufficiently established for the Lender to feel comfortable making loans in the area, so the Loan would not be approved.

"But the Loan was already approved," she said.

"No," said the Loan Officer, "you were pre-approved."

"But nothing changed," she said, "I gave you all of the information you asked for, and you said that was everything that you needed."

"Yes," he said, "that was all I needed, but the Committee makes the decision."

"Who the Hell is the 'the committee'," she asked.

"The Loan Committee. It's made up of the Bank's Board of Directors. They meet once a month, along with all of the Loan Officers. The Committee must approve the loans," the Loan Officer said.

Alice was totally confused. "I thought you approved the loans."

"No," he said, "I pre-approve you for a loan."

Alice was unable to arrange other financing in time.

She lost her $20,000 Earnest Money Deposit, and she had to move out of her Townhouse, because the new owner had already leased it to someone else.

WHAT SHOULD HAVE HAPPENED

Same scenario as before.

Alice owned a Townhouse in a row of

Townhouses that were gradually being bought up and turned into rentals.

Some of the activity in the area was not what she was accustomed to, and she was not enjoying her lifestyle as much as when she bought there a few years ago.

She was thinking of selling, and buying a house closer to her job.

Then she received a decent offer from the owner of the adjacent property, a Real Estate Investor who also owns some of the other Townhouses.

She found the perfect property to buy, in a new development, and at a good price.

She went to her Lender and applied for a loan.

But in this scenario, she told the Lender that she required a Loan Commitment Letter, so that there would be no question that she would actually be getting the loan.

Her Lender refused, saying that it was not their policy to provide a Loan Commitment Letter, that they would offer "pre-approval," which Alice knew meant nothing.

So, she had to go to four other Lenders, with the same results, before she found Premier Lending, a company that offered almost exactly what she wanted.

Premier Lending explained that the Loan Commitment Letter is actually called "Conditional Loan Approval," or "TBD Approval" because the property on which the loan will be made has not been identified. The property is "to be determined" – "TBD."

The document entitled Conditional Loan Approval is about four pages long.

The Conditional Loan Approval explains that the loan will have two sets of requirements that must be satisfied by the Borrower. This is the "conditional" part of the Conditional Loan Approval.

One set of requirements is called "Prior To Docs" conditions.

In a situation like this, when a Lender is ready to close on a loan, they notify the Closer (we are using a Title Company) to go ahead and order the Loan Documents from the Attorney.

The "Prior To Docs" conditions are conditions that the Borrower must meet before the Lender is satisfied and ready to order the Loan Documents to close the loan.

The other set of requirements is called "Prior To Close" conditions. You might also see these referred to as "Prior To Funding."

These are conditions that must be met before the Lender turns loose of the money, such as having the property put into the name of the Borrower, having a lien on the property created in favor of the Lender, etc. Most of these will be satisfied by the documents provided by the Title Company or the Lender, and signed at Closing.

So at this point, the loan has still not been approved.

That step requires a human being to study the file, and provide "Underwriting Approval."

What Alice has is Conditional Loan Approval, which is a letter that states that the loan will definitely be made if certain conditions are met, such as the Appraisal must be at least $X, and if it is not, Alice can increase the Down Payment to reduce the Loan Amount to $X, but the loan will definitely be made.

A Conditional Loan Approval is a binding commitment from the Lender to make the loan.

It is considered to be as good as cash in the real estate community.

Premier Lending explains to Alice that the approval that she has will eventually expire, along with the guaranteed interest rate, so it is critical that she get started right away with satisfying the requirements.

But before you get to the specific requirements, there are some general requirements that are common to all loans, such as:

1.) proof of mortgage insurance,

2.) title policy commitment,

3.) appraisal showing a value of at least a certain amount, and

4.) a termite inspection.

So, Alice went immediately and put the property under contract, including in the contract the condition that her financing must be approved, just to cover the unforeseen situations.

Then she took the Sales Contract to the local Title Company, and wrote a check for the Earnest Money to the Title Company, and she ordered an Owner's Title Policy Commitment and a Mortgagee's Title Policy Commitment.

Alice then went across the street to the insurance agency and ordered a mortgage insurance binder on the property.

When she got back to her office, she called a local Appraiser and ordered an Appraisal on the property, and called a local termite company and ordered a termite inspection on the property.

Some of these items are usually the responsibility of the Seller of the property, but Alice has more at stake here than the Seller has, and she is maintaining control. She has told the Seller that she is taking care of these items, and keeping the Seller in the loop on the progress.

While she is waiting for these items to be completed, she starts dealing with the first set of requirements, the "Prior To Docs" conditions.

In real life, the list that you might receive from the Lender will constantly change, depending on the condition of the economy, and the financial policies of the Lender, but could include:

1.) Pay stubs for the last 30-90 days,

2.) W-2s for the last two years, maybe three,

3.) Federal Income Tax Returns for the last two years, maybe three,

4.) 1099 Forms for any self-employment income or commissions,

5.) Documented dividends, stock earnings and other sources of income,

6.) Proof of bonus income,

7.) Pension statements,

8.) Cover pages of life insurance policies,

9.) Gift letter, if any portion of the Down Payment is from a gift,

10.) A signed copy of the Sales Agreement, and

11.) Written verification from the employer concerning salary and position.

Alice deals with all of these that pertain to her.

Then, at this point, Alice talks to the investor who offered to buy her Townhouse and works out the terms of a deal, and signs a Sales Agreement.

The Contract includes the contingency that it will only happen if she closes on the property that she is buying. It also provides her a certain number of weeks after closing to move out, and provides her an option to stay beyond that point on a month-to-month tenancy by paying a specified monthly amount, in case she has problems with the property that she is buying.

She provides a copy of this Sales Agreement to Premier Lending, to add to the other documentation.

As soon as all of the documents are in the loan file, Premier Lending will be in touch with the Title Company to verify that the "Prior To Docs" requirements have been met, and that the loan documents can now be ordered.

The Title Company will obtain them and provide the Lender with copies of the loan documents, and the Lender will approve them and provide a set of Closing Instructions for the Escrow Officer.

The Closing Instructions will contain the "Prior To Funding" requirements, and these requirements will be met by Alice prior to attending Closing, or at Closing, and will include obvious items such as filing a deed, retaining a lien in favor of the Lender, bringing property taxes current, etc.

The Title Company Closer will actually be doing these things.

The Closing takes place, either with the Seller and Alice at the closing table at the same time, or in some other manner.

The Lender is sent copies of some of the executed documents, and the Lender approves them, sends back a funding number, and wires the funds to the Title Company.

This completes the Closing.

Alice takes the keys to the property, and everything is done.

She decides to spend some time in the property to make sure that everything works, while she has the utilities turned on, and changes everything over.

Meanwhile, she contacts the Buyer of her Townhouse and has him proceed with that transaction, keeping in touch with each process to make sure that it is done correctly.

It turns out that there are no problems with the new property, just a few items to be replaced and some painting, which she is able to do before the Closing on the sale of her Townhouse, and she is actually ready to move on the day of that Closing.

Alice uses the Net Sales Proceeds from the Townhouse sale to replenish her financial accounts, and settles into her new life.

CONCLUSION

"Pre-Approved" is such a meaningless term that you will often receive a letter addressed to "Occupant" saying that you have been "Pre-Approved for 100% financing on a new" vehicle, along with no payments for three years, as well as a $5,000 Rebate.

Doesn't that tell you that it is a sham, and possibly a scam?

There is an even more misleading term used by Lenders, the "pre-qualified" term.

That means that you are not qualified. Is that supposed to be good news?

It, too, doesn't mean anything.

For real estate loans, all of this happens after you answer questions about your income, your credit score, your debts, and so forth. None of the answers are checked. But unless you admit to something that would disqualify you, you are told that you have been "pre-qualified" or "pre-approved."

In reality, nothing at all has happened.

Loan Officers and Mortgage Brokers are trained, when dealing with customers, to say "Yes" to everything up to the time they say "No."

They all do it, and they always have.

But you can control the situation by going to a Lender who is willing to do a Conditional Loan Approval.

It's as good as cash.

Most Lenders don't want to do a Conditional Loan Approval, because they don't like having to do what they promise. Instead, they like to come into work every day and make almost arbitrary decisions that are in their own best interest, but that affect people's lives in drastic ways.

Remember, this is a business relationship, and you are a businessperson.

If you don't establish, and maintain, your business position in the relationship, you are just sitting there, saying, "Please treat me fairly, I really don't know what I'm doing."

Don't do that.

You don't have to.

You can learn to do this.

Study the "Selected Resources" next.

If you still have questions, contact me.

SELECTED RESOURCES

MINIMUM MORTGAGE REQUIREMENTS

This is a good explanation of the different types of loans, and the different requirements for each one.

https://www.lendingtree.com/home/mortgage/minimum-mortgage-requirements/

EXPLANATION OF LOAN COMMITMENT LETTER PROCESS

This explains some of the conditions behind the conditional loan approval.

https://www.newamericanfunding.com/blog/the-conditions-behind-the-loan-approval/

EXAMPLE OF LOAN COMMITMENT LETTER

This is the best video I have seen explaining the process of obtaining a Loan Commitment Letter.

https://www.youtube.com/watch?v=BsOl_-W7w4w&t=3s

CHAPTER 3

ME OR LLC?

OVERVIEW

The most dangerous of all possible situations for Real Estate Investors, the idea that has been rambling around the blogs and podcasts for years, is the idea that it is perfectly fine if you borrow money to buy real estate, and then take that real estate out of your name by putting it into the name of an LLC.

This is a violation of the "Due On Sale" clause in your Mortgage or Deed of Trust, and will allow the Lender to accelerate all future payments to the current date, and declare the entire unpaid balance of your Mortgage immediately due and payable.

It can also be a criminal violation for "Hindering A Secured Creditor" and result in charges filed against you.

Even if neither of these things happen, there are numerous other possible problems, and you have just created a train wreck that is waiting to happen.

In any event, all possible outcomes are bad, and you really need to avoid it.

WHAT HAPPENED

Rob and Paul were brothers.

Rob, the older, went to college, majoring in Construction Management, and his younger brother, Paul, graduating High School the following year, went to two years of Community College, taking courses in Engineering, and then joined the Army, making it into the Corps of Engineers, and being assigned to the Military Construction Division.

So when they were ready to get on with their lives, they were ideally suited to do what they always wanted to do – build houses.

And they wanted to start their own company.

They had been planning to do this for some time, and each had saved $25,000 to put toward the venture.

Fortunately, they lived in a State with an LLC statute that was strong in its protection against liability for members.

So they formed an LLC, called it RAP, LLC, for "Rob And Paul," and each became a Member Manager.

They planned their first project, a 3 bedroom, 2 bath, double carport, 1,750 square feet, frame house in a decent area just inside the city limits.

The market value for similar properties, new construction, would be about $150,000.

They found a half-acre lot that could be cleaned up and landscaped to their needs for about $10,000. The utilities, foundation, and driveway would be another $10,000.

Their Materials List came in at $45,000.

They would do most of the work themselves, but knew they would have to use some sub-contractors like electricians, HVAC installer, and plumbers who had the required licenses, and they allocated $15,000 for this.

They thought they might need one or two "helpers," and set aside another $10,000 for this.

Altogether, they figured they could complete the project in 5 months for about $90,000.

They were excited when they went to their Bank with their LLC documents, the blueprints, and their projected numbers for construction.

The Loan Officer said the Bank would be happy to make them a Construction Loan, but in their personal names, not the LLC.

The Bank didn't make loans on residential real estate to an LLC. It was the Bank's policy, the Loan Officer said, and there was nothing he could do about it.

They offered to sign as Personal Guarantors on the loan, but the answer was still "No."

They were disappointed, and somewhat upset, and a little bit angry, but they felt that they had no choice, so they agreed.

The Loan Officer also said that Rob and Paul would have to own the lot free and clear, and pledge it as collateral for the loan. If they did, the Bank would loan 70% of the remaining $80,000 of needed construction funds.

So they bought the lot in their own names, using $10,000 of their operating cash. Then they signed the loan documents for the $56,000 loan, and the Bank held back $6,000 to cover their Closing Costs, leaving them a net of $50,000.

They had $40,000 of their cash remaining, but knew they would need $30,000 to cover the rest of the construction cost, so they pulled out $10,000 to hold as an emergency fund.

Their first Construction Draw was for $20,000. They used most of it for lot preparation and foundation and driveway. The rest, along with some of their own money, they used for buying framing material.

They were underway.

Almost immediately, they had their first problem.

One of the workers was busting the band on a stack of lumber when the stack collapsed and pinned him under it.

He was not seriously injured, and they took him to the Emergency Room and stayed with him while he was treated, and lost most of a day of work.

But it worried them to think that they were personally liable for his safety, and **if he had been seriously injured, they could be sued for a lot of money and not only lose their business, but possibly most of their personal assets.**

So they made their first mistake.

They decided to deed the lot to their LLC, and begin operating their business as a LLC.

They did not use an Assumption Deed, or Deed With Assumption, just a Warranty Deed. And the Deed did not mention the loan or the lien on the property in the "Reservation And Exceptions" section of the Deed, or in the "Encumbrances" section.

And they did not tell the Bank what they were doing, because they had read on all of the blogs that it didn't matter to the Bank.

Rob and Paul kept the bank accounts just like they were, because they had chosen to have the LLC taxed as a Partnership, and the accounts they were currently using were in both of their names, like the loan.

After the second Construction Draw of $20,000 and spending another $10,000 of their own money, about four months into the project, the LLC got a Certified Letter from an Attorney that stated that he represented a man named Harold Johnson, who was the son of Walter Johnson.

Walter Johnson had once owned the lot on which Rob and Paul were now building a house.

The Attorney explained that Walter Johnson had bought the lot before his first marriage, so it was his Separate Property. Harold was the son from this first marriage. And when his first wife died, the property remained Walter Johnson's Separate Property.

Then he married a second time and had a daughter, Lisa Johnson.

When Walter Johnson died, the daughter, Lisa Johnson, sold the property to Rob and Paul.

She filed an Heirship Affidavit in the county Real Property Records, which did not mention her father's first marriage or the son that he had, Harold Johnson. The Title Company accepted the Heirship Affidavit as proof of ownership and insured the Buyer and the Lender.

But now, the Attorney explained, his client actually owned half of the property, as one of the two heirs of Walter Johnson, who had died without a Will.

So what Lisa Johnson had actually sold to Rob and Paul was her half of the property.

It was quite a shock at first, but then Rob said, "Wait, didn't we get a Title Insurance Policy when we bought the lot? That should cover us for any problem about clear title to the property."

They were more relaxed when they took the letter, and a copy of their Owner's Policy of Title Insurance, to the Title Company, and showed both documents to the Manager, and asked, "What do we do about this?"

The Manager looked at the documents, and said, "These are not the same."

"Same what," Paul asked? "One is our Title Insurance Policy, and the other is a Letter from an Attorney."

"But the Title Insurance Policy is in your names, and the Letter is addressed to an LLC. Is this your LLC?"

"Yeah, well," Paul said. "We put the property into the LLC. We needed to be protected."

"You mean that you deeded the property to the LLC?"

"That's what we did, yeah."

"Then you no longer own the property?"

"No, but our LLC does."

"And your LLC is not a 'named insured' in the Title Insurance Policy."

"But we paid for a Title Insurance Policy on the property," Paul said.

"And it insured the two of you against loss due to a defect in the ownership of the property," the Manager said, "for as long as you two owned the property. But you no longer own the property."

"Are you saying the Policy is no good?"

"No, the Policy was perfectly good as long as you were the owners of the property. It lapsed when you disposed of the property. A Title Insurance Policy does not insure the next property owner."

After some more discussion, Rob and Paul saw that they had to accept the situation.

"So," Rob said, "is there anything at all you can do? Can you contact this guy?

"No," said the Manager, "we've never done business with your LLC, there is no existing business relationship, and we are not authorized to represent your LLC in a legal dispute. That would require a law license, which we don't have."

Things went downhill from there.

They made their second mistake.

They took the $10,000 in their Emergency Fund and, instead of hiring a Business Attorney to handle the matter for them, they hired a Trial Lawyer who advertised on TV that he was "the baddest bear in the woods," figuring they would be sued, since they didn't have any money left for a settlement.

His standard retainer was $25,000 so they had to sign a Promissory Note for another $15,000. But they were comfortable doing this because they thought this was Lisa Johnson's problem, not theirs, and the situation would end very quickly, and it would only cost a few thousand dollars in legal fees.

The Trial Lawyer immediately sent a letter to the Johnson Attorney denying the claim, demanding that he not take any action that might interfere with the completion of the construction, and threatening that if a lawsuit was filed, he would "tie it up in Court for three years."

The Johnson Attorney answered back with a copy of the lawsuit he had just filed, and a letter saying that he might have settled for the $5,000 representing half the sale price of the lot plus Mr. Johnson's legal cost, but since we weren't going in that direction, now the demand was for 50% of the $150,000 Fair Market Value of the completed construction on the lot, with no reduction for the debt against it, since Mr. Johnson did not sign for the loan, plus Attorney Fees and Court Costs.

He included a copy of a "Notice Of Lis Pendens" (Notice of Pending Litigation) which he had filed in the Real Estate Records of the County, and a copy of his letter to the Bank which included a copy of the Notice and an explanation of the lawsuit.

The Bank immediately froze the account of Rob and Paul, stopped the remaining funding of the loan, and sent them a Notice of Default on the loan under provisions of the "Due On Sale" clause of the Deed of Trust.

Construction was shut down.

Merchants began filing "Mechanic's Liens" on the property for the outstanding invoices that would not now be paid.

The Bank filed a Notice of Foreclosure on the property and sent a copy to the LLC, and to Rob and Paul.

The Bank filed a Claim with the Title Company on its Mortgagee's Policy of Title Insurance for the loan amount of $56,000. The Title Company agreed to pay the amount, less whatever the Bank could recover through Foreclosure on the property.

The Title Company sent a copy of their agreement letter to Rob and Paul, and put them on notice that they would be responsible for any payment that the Title Company had to make to the Bank.

The Bank then filed a criminal complaint against Rob and Paul under the Hindering a Secured Creditor statute, for transferring real estate that was being used as collateral for a loan.

At the Foreclosure Sale, the property sold for $65,000 in its partially-constructed condition.

After payment of the Bank loan secured by a first lien, and the outstanding invoices secured by the Mechanic's Liens, there was no money left from the Foreclosure Sale proceeds.

Rob and Paul were then sued by the Bank for the legal costs that the Bank had incurred, and they agreed to settle the Claim for the amount of funds left in their frozen account.

Rob and Paul fired their Trial Lawyer, and he sued them for the $15,000 unpaid Promissory Note, claiming that he had earned the entire amount of the Retainer, and they had to hire another Attorney to defend that lawsuit, and ended up having to borrow the money from their parents for the second Attorney's Retainer.

In the end, they each had to get other jobs, and sell their trucks to pay back their parents.

They considered themselves lucky that they only lost $50,000 and six months of their time, and a lot of sleep.

And fortunately, the County Prosecutor agreed to handle their criminal case for Hindering A Secured Creditor with the Deferred Adjudication Program, where they acknowledged the truthfulness of the allegations, and would have the entire case dismissed after six months and expunged from the record, if they were not charged with any offense during that period of time.

And that was their first venture into real estate investing.

WHAT SHOULD HAVE HAPPENED

Rob and Paul did everything correctly in the beginning, just like the first scenario.

But, at the point where the Bank refused to make a loan to the LLC, Rob and Paul looked elsewhere for funding.

They were feeling pretty confident.

They had a project that could be completed in five months, at a cost of $90,000 and it would have an after-built appraised value of $150,000.

They had $50,000 of their own money, but knew that they should not use all of it, and should not start spending any of it, or committing any of it, until they had guaranteed financing in place.

They thought that they probably already knew all of the Hard Money Lenders in the area, but they asked around just to make sure, and got some opinions.

They went to Clark HML and told them their situation and asked what they could do. They showed Clark all of their paperwork.

Clark said that they mostly made loans to Flippers who were buying and rehabbing distressed properties, but that they were now getting into financing of new construction, and they would be interested in making the loan.

Clark said that instead of the loan being based on the After Repair Value (ARV) of the property, like it would for a Rehabber, the loan would be based on the As-Completed Value (ACV) of the property, and that they would require both an As-Built Survey of the lot and house prior to construction, and an After-Completion Appraisal of the total property.

Assuming that the Appraisal came in at the expected amount of $150,000, Clark would loan 50% of this amount, which would be $75,000.

The interest rate would be 10%, not Annual Percentage Rate (APR), but for the six-month period of the loan, which would be an Annual Percentage Rate of 20%.

They would also charge two points, which is 2% of the loan amount, or $1,500.

Clark would require that RAP, LLC acquire the property, and bring $10,000 to the Closing to pay for it. They would do the Closings for the Purchase of the lot and for the Construction Financing in one Closing in order to save money.

Clark would get a Mortgagee's Title Policy for the $75,000 amount of the construction funds, and a First Lien on the property.

Also, Rob and Paul would each sign a Personal Guaranty to Clark HML on the loan.

They agreed, and Clark drafted the Loan Agreement, which they signed.

They then:

1.) Signed the Purchase Agreement on the Lot and took the Agreement to the Title Company, explained the terms of the transaction, and ordered an Owner's Title Policy Commitment and a Mortgagee's Title Policy Commitment. They also gave the Title Company an Escrow Deposit of $10,000. The Title Company explained, just for their information, that usually the second policy, for the Lender, in a transaction with financing, only costs an additional $100 more than the first policy, which is usually the Owner's Policy, but in this case the Mortgagee's Policy would be for $75,000 and the Owner's Policy would only be for $10,000, so the Title Company would base the first premium amount on the $75,000 Mortgagee's Title Policy, and the Owner's Policy would be the "additional policy" and would cost an additional $100. It was their first Real Estate Closing and they were learning things that they didn't know that they didn't know.

2.)   When they received the Title Policy Commitment from the Title Company showing title to the property was clear, they ordered an As-Built Survey and an After-Completion Appraisal.

3.) They took the Title Commitment, the Survey, and the Appraisal to Clark HML, and agreed on a date for closing.

4.) At Closing, the LLC received a Deed to the Lot, signed a Deed of Trust for $75,000 to Clark HML on the Lot, and received a $25,000 Advance from Clark.

At this point, Rob and Paul had spent $15,000 of their $50,000 on the purchase of the Lot, the Appraisal fee, the Survey fee, and Closing Costs.

So they still had $35,000 of their own money and the first $25,000 Advance of the Hard Money Loan.

They ordered the dirt work and foundation work on the Lot. They also ordered the framing material that they would need to get started. When the dirt work was done they ordered the cement work.

When the worker was injured busting the band on the stack of lumber, they went with him to the Emergency Room, verified his employment with their LLC, and provided information about the Workers Compensation Insurance Policy that they had been required to purchase since they were operating as a business entity instead of a sole proprietor.

They continued with construction, nearing the "drying in" point, when they got the letter from the Attorney notifying them that there was a claimant regarding partial ownership of the Lot.

They took the letter to the Title Company, filled out the Claim Form, and the Title Company turned it over to the Title Company Attorney to deal with.

Rob and Paul continued work on the project.

A month before scheduled completion, they put a For Sale sign in the yard, and began running ads, explaining that the Buyer could still choose the interior paint, light fixtures, floor coverings, and appliances.

They had a Sales Contract almost immediately for full price.

They ended up using all of the $75,000 of the Hard Money Loan, plus another $5,000 of their own money.

Closing costs were $5,000 and interest was $7,500.

So, their Net Sales Proceeds from the $150,000 was $62,500.

They had spent $10,000 of their own money for the Lot, another $5,000 for construction costs, and $1,500 for the two points up front for the loan, for a total of $16,500.

So their net profit was $46,000 for five months of work.

The $62,500 Net Sales Proceeds added to the $30,000 that they had left of their own funds gave them $92,500 operating capital for the next project.

They were already designing a Fourplex that they were pretty sure could be build for about $330,000 and have an After-Completion Value of about $550,000.

CONCLUSION

Buying your investment real estate in the name of your LLC is a great idea.

Trying to put investment real estate that you already own into your LLC when you have borrowed money in your own name to purchase that real estate, and created a lien in favor of the Lender, and doing it without the express approval of the Lender, is a terrible idea.

Period.

SELECTED RESOURCES

HINDERING A SECURED CREDITOR LAW

Committing the crime of "Hindering A Secured Creditor" usually involves selling an item of personal property like a car or boat on which you have borrowed money, but it can also include selling real estate with a lien against it.

And the penalty can range from a Misdemeanor to a Felony.

Here is a brief summary of the law in Texas. I just picked a State. Laws in other States will be different, and you should be able to find a law firm website that explains it.

https://saputo.law/criminal-law/texas/hindering-secured-creditors/#Hindering-Secured-Creditors-law

QUORA ANSWER EXPLAINING THE PROBLEM

I answered a Question on Quora regarding this situation, and it has over 21,000 views, so I assume it was helpful. I thought I would include it for you.

Here it is:

Question: Is it legal to hold the Deed to the property in the name of an LLC but finance the property in my own name?

Answer:

This is possibly the most misunderstood aspect of Real Estate Investing.

And yet, it is really the easiest to understand.

Here's how financing a property works, in simple terms.

1.) The lender loans you $100,000 to buy a $130,000 piece of property.

2.) The funds are sent to the Closing Agency to be given to the Seller of the property at closing.

3.) You provide the other $30,000 to be given to the Seller.

4.) At Closing, the property is deeded to you by the Seller, with a lien retained which the Seller assigns to your Lender.

5.) You sign a Real Estate Lien Note payable to the Lender.

6.) You sign a Deed of Trust to the Lender pledging a Security Interest in the property which allows the Lender to Foreclose on the property if you default on making the payments on the Note.

7.) Everyone goes home.

Now, let's look at your question.

No, you cannot.

The property must be in your name in order for you to create a lien on the property which the Lender requires in order to make the loan. No one else can create a lien on your property, and you can't create a lien on someone else's property.

It is actually a violation of Federal Banking Regulations for a Lender to make a loan that is not secured by sufficient collateral to protect the loan funds, because the presumption is that these funds are the deposits of the bank's customers, and they must be protected.

Once you receive the loan funds and pledge the property as collateral, you cannot transfer the property out of your own name, not even to an LLC in which you might be the sole member.

The LLC is a separate legal entity.

It would be no different from transferring title to the property to your next-door neighbor.

You no longer own it, and you borrowed $100,000 and pledged the property as collateral on the loan.

That is why the Lender has a clause in the Real Estate Lien Note that says if you transfer title to the property, the loan is immediately due and payable, and one of the default provisions of the Deed of Trust is triggered automatically, and Banking Regulations require that the Bank immediately collect the entire balance of the loan or that the property be posted for Foreclosure.

That's the law.

Banks are visited regularly by a group called "the Bank Examiners."

If they find that a Bank is ignoring "Due on Sale" clauses, there will definitely be heavy fines, and possibly more.

For you personally, there can be all kinds of horrible consequences if you do this anyway.

Say you transfer the property to your LLC, and it burns the next day.

Your insurance policy does not cover it because the policy is in your name insuring property that you own, and you no longer own it, and the LLC is not the "named insured."

If the Bank suffers a loss, you have now committed a crime called "Hindering a Secured Creditor" and/or "Fraudulent Conveyance."

Messing around with transferring title to secured property is treated very casually by a lot of people, but this is very serious business.

Sorry to be so pedantic, but it worries me to see this.

I hope this helps.

Good Luck.

Michael Lantrip, Attorney | Accountant | Investor

http://amazon.com/Michael-Lantrip/e/ B01N2ZRGUY

FREE BOOK CHAPTER

There is so much conflicting information, and a lot of information that is just plain wrong, on the internet, that I thought I would include a Chapter about the LLC from my book entitled "Your Best Business Entity For Real Estate Investing."

You will be using an LLC, or you will be doing business with others who are using an LLC, and you absolutely must understand everything that you can about an LLC.

I urge you to read this, and try to retain as much of it as you can.

I know it is long, but I think it will be very helpful to you.

If you want to skip it now, try to come back to it later.

CHAPTER 2

LIMITED LIABILITY COMPANY

OVERVIEW

The Limited Liability Company (LLC) is totally different from any other business entity that you might use.

And the LLC is the best thing to happen to Real Estate Investors since the creation of the Subchapter S Corporation which made it possible for individuals to have the protection of a C Corporation without the double taxation.

The Limited Liability Company is created by filing Articles of Organization.

The LLC is owned by the Members.

The ownership can be represented by membership units or just by percentages.

The LLC is managed by either the Members, or by one or more persons designated by the Members to be the Manager or Managers.

The agreement between the participants is a contract called the Operating Agreement.

Like the Partnership and the S Corp, the LLC is a Pass-Through Entity (PTE).

(See Chapter 10 of "Your Best Business Entity For Real Estate Investing" for an explanation of Pass-Through Entities.

With the LLC, you create a company which you use to do business, and in most States you will have no personal liability arising from the activities of the company, as long as you follow the law.

Now remember, each State has its own laws governing the formation, operation, and dissolution of the Limited Liability Company, which we will now call the LLC.

So, everything that I say should be confirmed by looking at your State law.

Most States have very good websites that will give you accurate and current information, and sometimes step-by-step directions for whatever you want to do.

In the Conclusion section at the end of this Chapter, I show you how to find the law for your State.

And I will only be dealing with Real Estate Investors who are doing "Buy and Hold" investing.

If you are flipping properties, you are not investing.

Flipping properties is operating a business, with inventory, and you are a dealer.

I have written an entire Chapter 13 in the book for you.

But you are probably also doing "Buy and Hold" as well, or should be, so this book will also be very beneficial to you.

FORMATION

There is no Federal law regarding the establishment and operation of a Limited Liability Company (LLC).

LLCs are created under State law, and therefore each one will be a little bit different.

But there are enough similarities that we can refer to all of the State statutes in general terms.

ARTICLES OF ORGANIZATION

An LLC is usually formed by filing Articles of Organization with the Secretary of State of your State.

In your State, the document might be called a Certificate of Organization or Certificate of Formation. But, since it is not a "certificate," we will call it Articles of Organization.

The State website for the Secretary of State will have a form with blanks that you can complete and send in with the fee. Or you can use the form as a guide, and draft your own.

A few states require that before you can file your Articles of Organization, you must file a public notice of your intent to do so in the local newspaper.

One person, referred to as the Organizer, can file the papers even if there will be multiple owners.

The information required in the Articles of Organization will vary, but will certainly include:

1.) Name of the LLC.

2.) Address of principal business.

3.) Name(s) of the Member(s).

4.) Name and address of the Registered Agent.

5.) Whether the LLC will be managed by Members or by Managers.

Members can be of any nationality, and there is no limit on the number of Members.

If you intend to operate in a State other than the State in which you form your LLC, you will need to file the necessary documents in the State of operation in order to qualify as a foreign entity. And then you will be required to follow the laws of both States, the one where you formed the LLC, and the one where the LLC is doing business. Usually, the laws of the State of formation will govern the operation of your LLC, but not always. This is something that you need to find out.

The dual-State requirements might also include filing tax returns in multiple States, depending on the requirements of those jurisdictions.

The State where the LLC is formed will also have other laws with which the LLC laws must be coordinated, such as the Community Property laws.

There are nine States with Community Property laws.

1.) Arizona

2.) California

3.) Idaho

4.) Louisiana

5.) Nevada

6.) New Mexico

7.) Texas

8.) Washington

9.) Wisconsin

REGISTERED AGENT

One important decision that you have to make concerns your choice of a Registered Agent.

The Registered Agent is someone, or an Entity, that will be served with the copy of the lawsuit if you are ever sued. You might be tempted to save the fee of having someone else do this, and just act as your own Registered Agent. This is allowed if you are located in the State. But do you want to commit yourself to having a location that is open every business day of the year, as required by law? And do you want a Constable or Process Server showing up at your office when you are meeting with someone?

I recommend having a third party handle this.

The Registered Agent's office can also serve as the LLC's "corporate headquarters" if you don't have an office in the State of formation.

You can find a Registered Agent in the State of formation by going to www.registered-agent-information.com, an independent website that contains information on Registered Agents for each State.

OPERATING AGREEMENT

In addition to the Articles of Organization, even if you have only one member, you will need to draft an Operating Agreement.

The Operating Agreement is the heart of your business, and it is the reason that the LLC can be more powerful than any other platform for Real Estate Investing.

The Operating Agreement is the most important of all of your documents.

The Operating Agreement is actually not required

by the LLC laws of some States.

This is a huge mistake, and it demonstrates the low level of understanding of the business world by the politicians who created the laws, and their reluctance to listen to people with expertise and experience.

You must have an Operating Agreement.

You must have one even if you are a Single Member LLC, because later you might want to consider adding a Member, and you need to provide for that in the beginning.

When you draft the Operating Agreement, you want to make sure that you understand exactly how it will be used to control everything that happens in your LLC.

The Operating Agreement will lay out:

1.) Interest ownership of Members.

2.) Rights and responsibilities of Members.

3.) Type of Management.

4.) Allocation of profits.

5.) Manner of holding meetings and voting.

6.) Buyout provisions.

7.) Timeline for profit distributions.

8.) The voting power of Members and Managers.

9.) Limits on disposing of LLC interest.

10.) Member death and disability.

11.) Dispute resolution.

So, you have two decisions to make.

HOW TO DO IT

The first decision is whether to go to the State website and learn about the process of creating an LLC and then doing it yourself, or to pay an online service to do it.

My feeling is that if you actually intend to become a business professional, and are not just playing around, you need to learn all you can about LLCs, and then do the formation yourself.

An online service has no information, education, access, qualifications, or experience that would enable them to do this better than you.

In fact, they have less.

And if you don't do it yourself, you have to think about the fact that, at some point in the future, you could wake up one day and realize that you have about $400,000 of Equity, and about $700,000 of debt obligation inside your LLCs, and you don't even understand how the LLCs were set up, or how they work, except the basics.

Do it right from the start.

Learn it, and do it.

But hold up on filing the documents for now.

The second decision you will make concerns your Operating Agreement.

Don't do it yourself.

Learn what an Operating Agreement is, and what it does, and then find an

Attorney who practices Real Estate Law, and who has Real Estate Investors as clients.

Know before you go in for your appointment what you want in your Agreement.

Make a list, make a copy.

Then go through the list with the Attorney.

Ask questions, and then ask the Attorney for suggestions.

I think you will be pleasantly surprised to discover what you can do with your Operating Agreement.

After you have the Operating Agreement created for your first LLC, if you continue to use the same Attorney, the Operating Agreement for subsequent LLCs should cost less each time.

You might even get lucky and find an Attorney who will create an Operating Agreement in which most of the variable information will be contained on attachments which will be referenced in the document as "...as described on Exhibit A which is attached hereto and incorporated herein for all purposes."

A new Operating Agreement can be created much easier.

When you have finished the consultation regarding the Operating Agreement, show the Attorney the documents that you intend to file in order to form the LLC, and go over the documents with him.

Ask questions, and then ask for suggestions.

And I promise you, when your LLC sells the investment property in the future, and you make $170,000 profit, you will not be complaining about the money you paid the Attorney to do it right in the beginning, and you probably willnever know how much time and money you saved by doing it right.

FINANCING

The LLC must have money and equipment to operate.

It does not usually start with a bank loan like some other Entities.

The financing will usually come from the future Members of the LLC.

The members will contribute:

1.) cash,

2.) property,

3.) personal services, or

4.) a promise to contribute cash, property, or personal services in the future.

In return for these "Capital Contributions," the LLC Member will receive a percentage of ownership called "Capital Interest."

The LLC can describe the ownership in terms of "membership units" or "ownership percentage."

If membership units are used, these must be described in the Operating Agreement, such as creating 1,000,000 units, and then an investor who puts in 25% of the Capital Interest would receive 250,000 membership units. But this can get cumbersome.

If the LLC is set up for ownership percentage, which most of them are, the same Member would just be referred to as having 25% ownership percentage, or 25% Capital Interest.

If a Member owns a 25% Capital Interest, that means that he is entitled to 25% of the net sales proceeds if the LLC itself were sold. And if the other Members wanted to buy him out, they would pay him 25% of the total value of the LLC on the books.

Whether or not his 25% Capital Interest would also mean that he will receive 25% of the LLC income and losses depends on the terms written into the Operating Agreement.

CAPITAL CONTRIBUTIONS

Whether the Member contributes cash, property, or services is critical, for the individual Member personally, and possibly for the other Members.

The Member will create different tax situations with the IRS for himself, and possibly other Members, depending on whether he contributes cash, property, or services.

CASH

For the Member who contributes cash, this is not a taxable event, and does not have to be reported on his personal tax return, and no tax liability is incurred. If he contributes $25,000 and receives a 25% Capital Interest, that establishes his tax basis in his Capital Interest at $25,000. If the other Members buy him out a year later for $30,000 before anything else happens to change his Capital Account, he has a $5,000 Capital Gain, which he will report on his tax return and pay taxes.

PERSONAL SERVICES

For the Member who receives his Capital Interest in return for his personal services, the situation is different.

The Member who receives a 25% Capital Interest valued at $25,000 in return for 100 hours of services already performed, and a promise of 400 more hours to be performed, has received "payment for services" under the IRS definition, and is liable for ordinary income taxes on the entire amount.

PROPERTY

For the Member who receives a Capital Interest in return for property, this is a special situation which I cover below in "Contributing Owned Real Estate."

MEMBER INCENTIVES

There is a greater enticement for Members of the LLC to invest in an LLC than there is for Partners to invest in a Partnership or Shareholders to invest in a Corporation, because each Member of the LLC can receive different benefits, income, and ownership, from those of other Members.

With an S Corp, when the income flows through to the Shareholders and is reported on the Schedule K-1 (1120S), the profits and losses are allocated in accordance with the ownership percentages of the Corporation.

If you own 25%, then you are allocated 25% of the profit, or 25% of the losses.

However, the Operating Agreement of the LLC can handle allocations in a flexible manner, without regard to ownership percentages, referred to as Unequal Allocation.

You might have someone interested in becoming a Member who wants to have losses allocated to him, so that he can deduct the amount from other like income, and avoid paying taxes on that other income.

Or you might have someone who requires a guaranteed return, before the remainder of the LLC income is allocated to the other Members.

The unequal or special allocation is allowed, but must have a "substantial economic effect," according to the IRS. The IRS says the allocation cannot be only to reduce the Taxpayer's tax obligation.

However, they realize that in most cases, this is the only reason for doing special allocations, and they allow it as long as it has a reasonable business purpose, and as long as all of the taxes tied to the LLC income are being paid by someone.

There are some special requirements regarding each Member's Capital Account and Basis, which I cover below in Bookkeeping.

MANAGEMENT

The Operating Agreement will provide the manner in which the LLC will be managed.

The two possibilities are:

1.) Member Managed, in which all of the Members take part in managing the LLC.

2.) Manager Managed, in which the Members agree on who will do the managing.

Some States require that the designation be made in the Articles of Organization, but the details should always be put into the Operating Agreement.

Under the LLC laws in most States, all Members are equally responsible for the management of the LLC.

This is the "default" classification of "Member Managed."

The Operating Agreement can provide for a different arrangement, and this is one of the most important items in the Operating Agreement.

The different arrangement is the arrangement known as "Manager Managed."

The Members choose one or more persons to manage the LLC, resulting in either single management or team management. A non-Member can be chosen as the single manager or as one of the team managers.

Any Member signing the Operating Agreement must understand that if he is not the single Manager, or one of the Managers, he is giving up his right to take part in the management decisions regarding the LLC.

Most of the business disputes that I have seen in the past 30 years involved management disputes, some of them resulting in lawsuits that went on for two or three years, many ending in Bankruptcy for the company, and sometimes for one or both of the individuals.

This is one of the three most important items that you will put into your Operating Agreement, along with ownership division and allocation of income.

Of course, many States have laws (and a good Operating Agreement has provisions) that a Member will always have the right to remove a Manager. If you do not want to be forced to follow the terms of the State law in this regard, the Operating Agreement should spell out exactly what the right is, how and when it can be exercised, and the process for doing it.

It might also be a good idea to provide that the Manager(s) serve for one year, and then must be appointed again.

OPERATING THE BUSINESS

You will operate the business in the most efficient and profitable way you can.

How you do that, and what you will be allowed or required to do, will be detailed in the Operating Agreement of the LLC, and will depend on the type of management you choose.

You should start out with a strong Operating Agreement, and as you go along, and find items that need to be improved, you should amend the Operating Agreement.

It is very important to understand that the LLC can be legally bound to any contract or transaction entered into by any Member in a Member Managed LLC, and by any Manager in a Manager Managed LLC.

Major decisions should only be made at a meeting of the Managers, either a regularly-schedule meeting or one called for the purpose, a "special meeting."

Minutes of the meeting and the votes should be recorded.

The Operating Agreement should spell out when the meeting should be held, who can call a meeting, how notice of the meeting is given, how the voting takes place, what constitutes a quorum, and how many votes are required to pass a proposal under consideration.

Although the State laws do not usually require annual meetings, and your Operating Agreement does not have to contain such a provision, it is a good idea for one of the Members to request a Special Meeting at least annually for the purpose of updating, reviewing, and summarizing operations.

This is not only the responsible thing to do, but it will prevent anyone from raising a dispute later and saying, "I didn't know."

Restrictions should be placed on the transfer of Capital Interest in the Operating Agreement.

The Operating Agreement should state that the recipient of a transferred Capital Interest, called the Assignee, regardless of how the Capital Interest was acquired, only receives the "economic interest," which is the distribution of the income.

The Assignee does not receive the management rights, voting rights, or membership rights. You can provide that full membership can be granted to the Assignee by either a majority vote, or a unanimous vote, of the other members.

A SMLLC can add a second Member, or additional Members, as provided for in the Operating Agreement.

This will usually be done by the single Member in a Single Member LLC selling some of his ownership units to one or more persons or Entities, or the LLC itself will just issue additional ownership units and sell them to the new Members.

If a single Member sells units, this will be a taxable transaction, and might require the Member to report the sale and pay taxes.

The LLC selling new units is not a taxable event.

The new Member or Members will sign the Operating Agreement, or an

Amended Operating Agreement will be drafted for all Members to sign.

And finally, you should remember that when you are signing documents for the LLC, the signature line should say:

Acme Widgets, LLC

By: _____

John Doe, Member

This will give notice that you're not signing as an individual, but that you are signing for the LLC in you capacity as an agent for the LLC.

BUYING REAL ESTATE

The LLC should be created first, and then the real estate should be purchased by the LLC.

You should not purchase the real estate first, and then try to put it into the LLC.

For the reasons why you should not do that, see the following Section on Contributing Owned Real Estate.

FINANCING

The LLC is a separate Business Entity and should purchase the real estate and hold the real estate in the name of the LLC.

If the LLC is new, and it probably will be, and you are not paying cash for the property, it will be difficult, and maybe impossible, to get a mortgage in the name of the LLC.

However, there are Lenders who will loan money to the LLC and take the real estate as security on the loan, if the Loan-to-Value (LTV) ratio is low enough.

It might require a larger Down Payment by the LLC, and it might require a guarantee of the loan by one or more Members of the LLC.

But don't be afraid of guarantees, and just remember that there are two types of guarantees.

The first is a Loan Guarantee, where you sign an agreement with the Lender that says if the loan goes into default, the Lender will simply notify you, and it is your responsibility to deal with the problem. This is virtually the same as getting the loan yourself.

The second is a Guaranty Agreement, where you guarantee the Lender that you will cover any loss suffered if the loan goes into default, and the Lender forecloses, and does not realize enough net proceeds to pay the loan.

The second is obviously better.

But if the Lender insists that you sign the Note, look for another Lender.

SEGREGATING PROPERTY

You should always hold each of your rental properties in a separate LLC.

If you believe that $1,500 is too much to pay for the most important item in your entire real estate investing plan, then you don't understand yet what matters and what doesn't.

If you have been investing for a few years, and you have three properties, all in the same LLC, and one tenant has an accident on your stairs, and is paralyzed for life, the lawsuit will probably result in a Judgment in the millions of dollars.

The lawsuit will be against the LLC, as will the Judgment, and all of the properties will be foreclosed on and sold to pay toward the Judgment lien.

Even without considering the possibility of a lawsuit, there are other reasons to put each property into its own LLC.

The income and losses from the rental real estate are passive in nature.

If you put only one property into each LLC, the losses from one LLC are deductible from the income of the other LLCs, shielding that income from taxation.

This significant advantage might allow you to take on a good long-term investment that will incur early losses, when other investors might not be able to do so.

It also allows you to balance your risks, as well as isolating them.

When the downturn comes, and some of your investments start to go belly-up, you have built a firewall between the shaky investments and the better investments that might survive. If you have to chuck the bad ones, you can still save the good ones.

If you had them all in one LLC, they might all go down.

To look at it from the opposite perspective, there is really no good reason to put all of you properties into one LLC, except to save money. And if you can't afford the best liability protection available, maybe you shouldn't be in the business.

Risking everything you own to save $1,500 just does not make sense.

CONTRIBUTING OWNED REAL ESTATE

As I discussed above in FINANCING, one of the ways that a Member can receive a Capital Interest in the LLC is in return for property.

This can be a tax nightmare!

PRACTICAL CONSIDERATIONS

But first, before we get to the tax considerations, there are simple, practical reasons why you should not transfer title to real estate to the LLC in return for your Capital Interest.

1.) The property probably has debt, for which you are personally liable, and which is being secured by a lien on the property, title to which is in your name.

You cannot transfer the title without transferring the debt, and the Lender is not likely to agree to that.

If the Lender does agree to it, the Lender would probably require that you remain liable on the debt, or a Guarantor for it, and that means that you are now responsible for a share of the LLC's debt, and that causes other IRS regulations to kick in.

2.) When you acquired the property, you obtained an Owner's Title Insurance Policy which guarantees that the property has clear title, and promises to cover any losses caused by defective title.

If the property has a mortgage, when you bought it, the Lender received a Mortgagee's Title Insurance Policy which insured the Lender against loss for the same causes related to title.

When you transfer ownership, both of these insurance policies cease, and neither the LLC nor the Lender is covered for things like a gas pipeline easement being discovered under the property.

If you decide to go ahead anyway, let's look at the tax nightmare ahead.

TAX CONSIDERATIONS

Usually, the property that you transfer to the LLC has gone up in value since you acquired it. (You would have to wonder why the LLC is accepting real estate if it is going down in value.)

Therefore, you are transferring what is called "appreciated property."

If you bought the property for $25,000 and it is worth $100,000 at the time of transfer, you will receive a Capital Interest equal to $100,000.

But, your tax basis in your Capital Interest of $100,000 will be $25,000.

The transfer itself does not trigger the Capital Gains tax. But you will have to pay the Capital Gains tax when you sell your Capital Interest, or when the LLC is sold.

However, if you receive a profit distribution from the LLC within two years of the date of the property transfer, you might owe the Capital Gains tax at that time.

You might also owe the Capital Gains tax if the LLC itself sells the property you contributed, or distributes the property to another Member.

The situation becomes even more complicated if you transfer property to the LLC and the property has mortgage debt attached to it.

This is not a problem for a Single Member LLC, although there are strong reasons not to do it, as described above.

But there are immediate tax consequences for a Member who transfers property with mortgage debt to the Multi Member LLC.

When they do, the mortgage debt is allocated among all LLC Members, including the transferor.

This has the effect of increasing each Member's basis in his Capital Interest, which will decrease his Capital Gains tax later when he sells his interest.

But it can have an immediate, and negative, effect on the transferor Member.

If he is in a Multi Member LLC with four other members and he transfers real estate with a FMV of $150,000 and which still has a $100,000 mortgage balance, that personal debt will now be shared among the five Members.

That means that he is no longer liable for $80,000 of the mortgage.

The result is that he will have $80,000 of personal "debt relief," and the IRS will consider this taxable as ordinary income to the transferor if the debt being transferred exceeds the total of:

a.) the transferor's share of the LLC debt, and

b.) the basis of the real estate being contributed.

If the transferor had a $70,000 basis in the transferred property, this is a taxable event.

Not only that, but he received a $150,000 Capital Interest when he transferred the property, so when he sells his Capital Interest, he will owe Capital

Gains on another $80,000 even if he doesn't sell it for more than $150,000.

If he does, he will owe Capital Gains on that profits as well.

SELLING REAL ESTATE

The real estate is owned by the LLC, and will have to be sold by the LLC.

The Operating Agreement of the LLC will detail who has the authority to make the decision to sell the real estate, and will describe the steps necessary to accomplish it.

The Net Sales Proceeds from selling the real estate will be owned by the LLC.

The "nature" of the income, for tax purposes, will be Capital Gains.

If the real estate was held for a year or less, the Capital Gains will be Short-Term Capital Gains.

If the real estate was held for at least a year and a day, the Capital Gains will be Long-Term Capital Gains.

Since the LLC is a Pass-Through Entity (PTE), the income will come to the Member or Members as Capital Gains to be reported on their individual tax returns.

PROVIDING SERVICES

The services that you will be providing to the LLC as a Member Manager will not be paid for with a paycheck.

Your LLC will operate as a Pass-Through Entity (PTE) and all of the income, deductions, credits and other items will pass through to the Members and be reported on their individual tax returns.

This will represent their compensation for managing the business, as well as the return on their investment of funds and of time putting the company together.

DISTRIBUTIVE SHARE

You should become familiar with a term that the IRS uses in its rules and publications, because you will see it a lot. "Distributive share."

The Distributive Share is the amount of an LLC's annual profits and losses that will be allocated to each Member.

Usually, the Distributive Share is the same as the Member's Capital Interest.

For Example, if four people each own 25% Capital Interest in the LLC, each would be allocated 25% of the LLC's profits and losses.

But the Operating Agreement can provide for a different allocation, and this is called "unequal allocation."

For Example, one of the four Members has 30 years experience operating the type of business and has been very successful, and will be more valuable, and he will be assigned 40% of the profits and losses, and the other three Members will be assigned 20% each.

The IRS requires that the Unequal Allocation must have a "substantial economic effect," in addition to any effect on the Member's tax liability, but this applies primarily in situations where one Member is allocated all of the losses so that he can deduct them from his other similar income. If you are doing this, it would be a good idea to consult an expert. It is complicated.

PAID COMPENSATION

It is possible in the Operating Agreement to have conditions whereby one of the Members receives a Special Allocation in the nature of an Unequal Allocation, but actually before the computation of the income which is subject to the Unequal Allocation.

So you have a Special Allocation, and then an Unequal Allocation of the rest.

There might be one Member Manager who shows up every day, executes the business plans, and ensures that tasks are completed, all things that the other Members do not do, and he is therefore entitled to compensation.

But to deal with this situation with a Special Allocation, as cool as it sounds, can really cause problems among the Members. There is a very high likelihood that at least one other Member will feel that the compensated Member is not spending sufficient time to justify the Special Allocation of income, and all of the Members will constantly be aware that the one Member's payment is coming from LLC income, before they get their share.

You could even have a situation where the Special Allocation takes up all of the income, and the other Members get nothing.

A much better solution is to have the Member who is providing these services to actually be an employee of the business, totally separate from his status as a Member and his position as a Member Manager.

He will receive a salary, and it will be treated as a regular business expense, just like the telephone, internet service, office supplies, etc., and when the LLC income is calculated, it will be distributed the way that everyone agreed in the Operating Agreement.

BOOKKEEPING

Bookkeeping has two purposes in your business.

The primary purpose of Bookkeeping is to keep track of the income and expenses, and to file the required tax documents.

You can learn to do this yourself fairly easily, or you can just find a good Bookkeeper to start with, and maintain frequent communications so that you always know where you are.

But the secondary purpose of Bookkeeping for LLCs, LPs, and S Corps is to keep track of each owner's Capital Account.

This requires following the standard rules of accounting (which you are probably familiar with, whether you realize it or not), but also following the specific IRS regulations (with which you are probably not familiar).

A Capital Account shows the amount of money put into the company by the investor/owner, plus his allocated portion of the profits, and minus the distributions that he has received.

If the Capital Account goes negative, the owner can be required to bring it to zero.

And, of course, he must bring it to zero before he can sell his interest, or in the event of a dissolution of the entity.

Capital Account reconciliation might not be something that you want to be spending your time doing, and might be a good reason for you to hire a Bookkeeper.

If the Operating Agreement provides for unequal allocation of the income, deductions, credits and other items, the Bookkeeping must take this into account.

You must also keep track of Basis. "Basis" is generally what you paid for an asset.

For LLCs and LPs, the concept of "Basis" can become complicated.

You will have "Inside Basis" and you will have "Outside Basis."

First, Inside Basis.

The Entity will purchase an asset. The purchase price is the Entity's basis in the asset. The Entity might spend money to improve the asset. This cost is added, creating a new Basis. The Entity might be entitled to deduct a portion of the Basis as a "Depreciation Allowance." This is deducted, and will create a new Basis.

This is the Inside Basis, the Basis that the Entity has in the assets.

Now, Outside Basis.

The Owners of the Entity will also have a Basis in the ownership of the Entity that they acquire, their ownership interest.

If there are two Owners and they each invest $30,000 to become partners in the Entity, each Owner would have a $30,000 Basis in their interest in the Entity.

The Outside Basis can be increased if the Entity secures a loan and the loan is personally guaranteed by the Owners. This is different from an S Corp, where the Outside Basis can only be increased if the Owner loans the money to the Entity.

LIABILITY

"Limited Liability Company" does not mean that the company has limited liability.

The company is completely liable for all of its activities. And if those activities result in an injury to someone, and that person obtains a judgment against the company, the company's asset can be taken to satisfy the judgment.

The "limited liability" in Limited Liability Company refers to the fact that the owners/ investors (Members) of the LLC are not liable for the obligations of the LLC, except to the extent of the amount that they have invested.

That is because this invested amount now belongs to the LLC, and if it is lost and there are still unsatisfied obligation of the LLC, the owners/investors are not liable for those obligations.

The "liability" for the operation of the "company" is "limited" for the owners/investors to the amount that the owners/investors have put into the LLC.

ENTITY

The Limited Liability Company is responsible for its own debts and obligations.

The LLC can be sued if it does not pay these debts and meet these obligations, and the assets of the LLC can be sold to satisfy the debts and obligations.

But the Members are not liable.

However, a claimant can attempt to "pierce the veil" of the company, ignore its existence, or dissolve it, and hold the individual Members liable under certain circumstances.

That discussion is very complicated, and is different for each State, because it depends on the law of each individual State, and we don't have the space for a complete discussion here.

It is a rare occurrence to "pierce the veil," and usually involves wrongdoing on the part of a Member.

It gets more attention and publicity than is warranted by the frequency of its occurrence.

I refer you to Chapter 14 on Charging Orders in "Your Best Business Entity For Real Estate Investing" for some understanding of how outside liability can lead to dissolving the LLC.

INDIVIDUAL

The Members of the LLC are not liable for the debts and obligations of the LLC, except, of course, for any amount of debt that they have personally guaranteed.

Also, an individual Member might be held liable for any negligent personal acts that result in damages being awarded against the LLC. However, other LLC Members will not share the liability. It will only be assessed against the LLC and the responsible Member. The LLC insurance policy might or might not cover the negligent act of the individual Member.

And the interest owned by the Member in the LLC cannot be taken to satisfy the Member's individual obligations, except in a few States, and in narrow circumstances in some other States.

There is one way that an individual who is a Member of an LLC can be held liable for the obligations of the LLC, and that concerns the IRS.

If you are the individual responsible for sending in the money withheld from employees' paychecks, and you fail to do so, you will be held personally liable by the IRS, even if you were told to do so by the other Members.

And this is not just a fine.

This can become a Federal Tax Lien on everything you own or ever will own, including wages, until it is paid.

TAXATION

The two main reason for using an LLC are protection against personal liability, and control of your tax obligations.

After you create the LLC and are receiving the protection against personal liability, you then get to decide how you want to be taxed by the IRS.

FEDERAL

There are actually two ways in which you can tell the IRS how you want to have the LLC treated for tax purposes.

The first way is to do nothing.

If you do nothing, and you are the only Member of the LLC, the IRS will treat you for tax purposes as an individual taxpayer and you will report your business activities on your personal tax return, either Schedule E or Schedule C.

The IRS considers the LLC "a disregarded entity."

If the LLC has more than one Member, and the Members do nothing, the LLC will be treated for tax purposes as a partnership.

The second way to tell the IRS how you want to have the LLC treated for tax purposes is to file Form 8832, Entity Classification Election.

For a Single Member LLC, the Member can elect to be treated as "an association taxed as a corporation" as the language of the Form says. This means that you are electing to be treated as a C Corporation.

If you want to be treated as an S Corporation, you must follow the filing of Form 8832 with filing Form 2553, Election by a Small Business Corporation and that will make you an S Corp.

NOTE: there is language in the Form 8832 Instructions that seems to say that if you are an LLC and you only file the Form 2553 without filing the Form 8832, you will be "deemed" to have first filed the Form 8832. But I don't like it, and I think it could cause big problems under certain circumstances. I strongly recommend filing both forms. I have a more complete explanation below.

For a Multiple Member LLC, you can file Form 8832 and Form 2553 just like a Single Member LLC.

At the federal tax level, your LLC will not file a tax return and pay taxes, unless you file Form 8832, Entity Classification Election, and elect to be taxed as a C Corporation, and do not also file Form 2553, Election by a Small Business Corporation.

But your LLC might still be required to file a federal income tax return, and pass the income through to the owners, since the LLC is a Pass-Through Entity (PTE).

ENTITY

Form 8832 is not specifically for LLCs.

According to the IRS, it is for use by any "eligible entity" to "elect how it will be classified for federal tax purposes, as a corporation, a partnership, or as an entity disregarded as separate from its owner."

The LLC is an "eligible entity" entitled to file Form 8832.

If you are a single owner, the form says:

"You can elect to be classified as an association taxable as a corporation or to be disregarded as a separate entity." By "you" it means the LLC.

For an LLC with more than one owner, the form says:

"You can elect to be classified as a partnership or an association taxable as a corporation."

The Instructions to Form 8832 say that if you do not file anything, the single owner LLC will be classified as a disregarded entity, and the multiple owner LLC will be classified as a partnership.

Then, at this point, I believe that the IRS has introduced confusion into the situation.

An Entity that wants to taxed as an S Corp should, I believe, reasonably take the first step of filing Form 8832 and "elect to be classified as an association taxable as a corporation" and then file Form 2553, Election by a Small Business Corporation to be taxed as an S Corp.

But in a small paragraph on page 2 of the Form 8832 Instructions, it says:

"An eligible entity that timely files Form 2553 to elect classification as an S corporation and meets all other requirements to qualify as an S corporation is deemed to have made an election under Regulations section 301.7701-3(c)(v) to be classified as an association taxable as a corporation."

Then, section 301.7701-3(c)(v) says:

"An eligible entity that timely elects to be an S corporation under section 1362(a)(1) is treated as having made an election under this section to be classified as an association, provided that (as of the effective date of the election under section 1362(a)(1)) the entity meets all other requirements to qualify as a small business corporation under section

1361(b). Subject to § 301.7701-3(c)(1) (iv), the deemed election to be classified as an association will apply as of the effective date of the S corporation election and will remain in effect until the entity makes a valid election, under § 301.7701-3(c)(1)(i), to be classified as other than an association."

There is nothing in the consent statement of Form 2553 signed by the owners informing the owners that they are "deemed" to have filed another, different, Form, and I think that if the S Corp status was ever lost, and the LLC was reverted to being a C Corporation, even though a Form 8832 was never signed under oath and filed by the owners, there could be problems.

Form 2553 is for use by "a small business corporation" and an LLC that has not elected corporate taxation status is not "a small business corporation."

I just don't understand why the IRS sets up this elaborate, confusing, convoluted, and very unclear process for being "deemed" to have filed Form 8832, when you can just file the damn Form in fifteen minutes, and not have any of this uncertainty.

I always file both Forms, but I admit that I am not aware of any recent cases where this has become an issue, so you can make up your own mind about whether to file only Form 2553 if you want to be taxed as an S Corp.

So, as you can see, the LLC will not pay Federal Income Taxes unless you first elect to be treated for tax purposes as a C Corporation, and then you do not file the Form 2553 Election to be treated as a Subchapter S Corporation.

(Or, in my opinion, you file Form 2553, and then lose your S Corp status.)

If you choose to be taxed as a C Corporation, you will file Form 1120, US Corporation Income Tax Return, and pay the appropriate amount of corporate tax, which is now 21% under the new Tax Cuts And Jobs Act. You will transfer the remainder of the income into a corporate account called Retained Earnings.

If you decide to pay a Dividend to the Shareholder(s), this is where it comes from.

But if you are an individual and you just create your LLC, and then do nothing about filing your Form 8832, Entity Classification Election, then you will receive the default classification, which is Disregarded Entity.

Being classified as a Disregarded Entity means that for purposes of reporting the income and paying the taxes, it is the same as if you owned the property in your individual name.

The rental income will be reported on your Schedule E, and the LLC will file nothing with the IRS.

If the LLC has more than one owner, it will be considered a Partnership.

The LLC will than file a Form 1065, US Return of Partnership Income, and then provide a Schedule K-1 (Form 1065) for each Partner, showing each

Partner's share of income, deductions, credits, and other items, which the Partner will report on his personal return.

I have a good discussion of the Form 1065 handling of Partners' Account in Chapter 6 Limited Partnership > Taxation > Federal > Entity.

If the LLC elects to be classified for tax purposes as an S Corp, it will file Form 1120S, US Income Tax Return for an S Corporation, which is similar to the

Form 1120 that is filed by C Corporations.

The Form 1120S will calculate the income, credits and deductions, and put them on a Schedule K-1 for each owner, and the individual owner will report the amount on their personal tax returns.

INDIVIDUAL

If you choose to have the LLC treated for tax purposes as a Disregarded Entity, the income and expenses will be reported on your Schedule E and the Net Income will be added to your Form 1040.

This income will be taxed as ordinary income at your individual tax rate.

The income will not be subject to Self-Employment (SE) Tax because it is considered to be passive income, and therefore unearned income.

If you elect to have your LLC treated as an S Corporation, you will receive a Schedule K-1 (1120S), which will give you all of the numbers to use on your tax return, along with instructions about where to put them.

If you perform services for the S Corp, you will have to be paid a reasonable salary, and that salary will be subject to withholding for Social Security and Medicare, half of which will be paid by the Corporation and half withheld from your check.

If your LLC has more than one owner, it will be taxed as a partnership, and you will receive a Schedule K-1 (1065) showing your share of the income, deductions, credits, and other items, which you will report on your personal income tax return.

If you are a Disregarded Entity, an S Corp, or a Partnership, the income that is passed through to you qualifies for the Section 199A 20% Qualified Business Income Exclusion.

You will not be able to form your LLC in a State that has no income tax, and thereby avoid paying State taxes where you reside.

Remember, the LLC is a Pass-Through Entity and you will report the income on your personal tax return.

And you are required to file your personal tax return where your "tax home" is, and that is your State of residence.

STATE

There are seven States which have no State Income Tax.

They are:

1.) Alaska,

2.) Florida,

3.) Nevada,

4.) South Dakota,

5.) Texas,

6.) Washington, and

7.) Wyoming.

The other States impose some type of tax on income.

The tax rates vary, and the exceptions, deductions, exemptions, and thresholds vary.

Most State will treat the LLC the say way that the IRS does for tax purposes, but might have some additional filing requirements.

You should go to your State's taxation website to find out.

ENTITY

Each State will treat LLC income differently, depending on how you elect to be taxed at the federal level.

Your State website will contain the information you need to deal with this.

INDIVIDUAL

Each State will treat LLC income differently, depending on how you elect to be taxed at the federal level.

Your State website will contain the information you need to deal with this.

CONCLUSION

The Limited Liability Company is the favorite business entity of most small businesses, but especially real estate investors.

The LLC is a total departure from the old way of doing business, and with the new Tax Cuts and Jobs Act, it is likely to become the overwhelming choice of the future.

In addition to what we have already discussed, there are three major advantages that the LLC has over other Entities.

FLEXIBILITY

You can use an LLC for almost any situation that your are likely to encounter as a real estate investor, and still not have to sacrifice benefits for anyone.

Whether your LLC has one Member, two or three Members, or 100 Members, you can write the Operating Agreement to do exactly what you want to do, the way you want to do it.

You can override almost all of the rules contained in the LLC statutes of your State.

ASSET PROTECTION

The LLC is the ideal way to own real estate, for two reasons.

The two reasons also provide dual liability protection.

If your real estate is owned by your LLC and there is an accident on the premises that results in a lawsuit leading to a large Judgment, the Judgment will be against the LLC, and not against you personally.

To satisfy the Judgment, on the assets of the LLC, the real estate, can be taken.

And the assets must be taken subject to the existing debt. When the assets are sold, the mortgage will be paid off.

The only thing you lose will be your Equity. And

if you are careful and make sure that you carry as much debt as possible on the real estate, this will prevent the LLC from even being sued in the first place, because there is not enough equity to justify the time and expense of a lawsuit.

The second scenario involves a lawsuit and Judgment against you, or another Member of the LLC, not the LLC itself.

The LLC is unique among Business Entities in this regard, because the real estate owned by the LLC cannot be taken by the holder of the Judgment Lien.

Also, the Member's ownership of his interest in the LLC cannot be taken to satisfy the Judgment Lien.

The only remedy available to the holder of the Judgment Lien is to have the Court award a Charging Order, which entitles the Judgment Lien holder to receive the distributions of income, if such distributions are made.

But the holder of the Judgment Lien, the recipient named in the Charging Order, will still be required to pay income taxes on the amount of the annual distributions, even if they are not distributed.

As you can see, this will likely prevent the Judgment Lien holder from even requesting a Charging Order.

And since the Judgment Lien holder does not receive the rights of the Member of the LLC, even with a Charging Order, and cannot take part in the operation of the company, there will probably not even be a lawsuit if you hold all of your assets in different LLCs.

RAISING CAPITAL

The general impression is that Startup Entrepreneurs and Investors only use C Corps for investing purposes.

This is true if the amounts are in the millions and multi-millions of dollars.

But for at least 90% of such projects, which are much smaller, the LLC is the perfect platform and Entity.

This is true for both the Entrepreneur and the Investor.

Investors love the "pass-through" nature of the Partnership tax treatment.

The income is passive income and not subject to the 15.3% Self – Employment tax, and up to 20% of the total might even be tax-free under Section 199A.

The losses are deductible from the Investors' other passive income, allowing them to actually deduct their investment from taxable income.

For the Entrepreneur, the Operating Agreement can be written so that Investors can get exactly what they want in return for their funds, so it is much easier to attract capital.

The LLC can have an unlimited number of Investors, and they can be located anywhere.

The LLC can even have different classes of Membership, some with voting rights and some without, some with the right to transfer ownership, some without.

The Entrepreneur can also provide in the Operating Agreement that he will be the sole Member Manager, and he will be able to run the project on his own instead of having to hold up every decision until all Members have been notified, have reviewed the material, and have held a meeting to vote their approval.

The LLC can be just like running your own project, using other people's money, without dealing with stock, or Limited Partnership interests, or using a scammy Trust.

I think I have provided everything you will need as a Real Estate Investor to make your decision about whether the LLC is the Best Business Entity for you, but there are always additional items that you want to know about.

The best place for you to learn about those things is your own State's website.

Go to www.statelocalgov.net.

In the left sidebar, click the down arrow for "Select Topic" and choose SOS (for Secretary of State).

You will be shown a list of the States. Scroll down to yours and click on the Secretary of State link.

Use the Search box to find what you need.

If you want to look at your State's law governing LLCs, or even another State's laws, go to soswy. state.wy.us/Business.

This is Wyoming's website, and it is the best one of its kind I have ever seen.

Under the Section "Maintaining Your Business" click on "50 States'

Business Information" and then click on your State in the map.

Well, I hope that was some help to you.

I know it was brief, but I think it contains all of the essential information that you need to understand the Limited Liability Company.

CHAPTER 4

SPEND CASH, DON'T SPEND CASH

OVERVIEW

If you are already established as a Real Estate Investor, then "cash" is probably not a problem for you.

Either you have your own cash, or you're in a position to borrow cash in an efficient manner, and under reasonable conditions.

However, if you're a newer investor, what you probably have in abundance is "time" instead of cash.

In <u>your</u> investing environment, cash is your scarce commodity.

Cash is the thing that will limit your activities.

Cash is the commodity that you must be careful to allocate efficiently.

One of the most-asked question by new real estate investors is "How much of my own money should I use?"

Well, only <u>you</u> can make that decision, because you are the only one with knowledge of all of the factors that go into the decision.

So, although I can't make that decision for you, I can <u>help</u> <u>you</u> make it by looking at a situation involving the use of cash in two different scenarios, and hopefully provide you some insight into the factors that you might want to consider.

WHAT HAPPENED

Harold and Mary just finished college and they were comfortable in their rented apartment near campus, where all of their friends lived.

They were each starting entry-level jobs in their chosen fields.

Mary's parents had died and left their home to her, and after probate of the estate, and selling the property, they had ended up with $160,000 cash.

They talked about how they could use the money to buy their own home instead of continuing to rent their apartment for $1,600 per month.

Or they could invest the money in rental real estate.

They discussed it, and decided to use the money to buy their own home.

They found a good property for $140,000 and they spent $20,000 fixing it up, resulting in a nice comfortable home with a Fair Market Value of about $175,000.

Then they concentrated on building their careers, able to live comfortably on their starting salaries, not having to worry about monthly rent payments.

Five years later, they were ready to move up to a bigger home.

Their $175,000 home had increased in value 6.7% per year, and is now worth $242,025.

If Harold and Mary decide to sell their home, they can do so without paying any Capital Gains tax on the $82,025 increase in value because of Section 121 of the Internal Revenue Code.

Section 121 says that if a husband and wife own a property and live in it as their primary residence for at least two years out of the five years prior to the date of the sale, they can exempt from Capital Gains taxation up to $500,000 of the profit.

So, in our first scenario, Harold and Mary started with $160,000 cash, and after five years, they have a house, free of debt, with a Fair Market Value of $242,025 and no Capital Gains liability if they cash out.

This represents a Return On Investment (ROI) of 51.27% for five years.

This measures their increase in Equity.

Their Cash On Cash Return (COCR) for their Equity is also 51.27% for five years, because their Equity was initially all cash.

WHAT SHOULD HAVE HAPPENED

Harold and Mary are prime customers for an FHA Loan, at only 3.5% Down Payment, and a low interest rate on a 30-year fixed Mortgage.

So let's see what happens if they do that.

They find a nice home in move-in condition for $175,000 that qualifies for the FHA Loan.

They make a Down Payment of $6,125. Their Closing Costs and other expenses are $3,875. They spend a total of $10,000.

Their Mortgage is $168,875 for 30 years, at 4% fixed, and their monthly payment is about $800.

After deducting their $10,000 of Acquisition Costs from the $160,000 cash that they started with, they have $150,000 remaining, and they decide to use it to buy three rental properties.

Each property is $165,000 and they pay $50,000 down on each.

The Mortgage on each property is $115,000 at 5%, amortized for 25 years, with a 5-year balloon.

Each payment is about $675 per month.

Each property rents for $1,600 and after paying all expenses, including property taxes, insurance, and note payments, they net about $450 on each one.

This Cash Flow from the rental properties covers the Note payment on their home, and gives them a $500 monthly cushion, which is usually spent on unanticipated expenses, or saved for later and spent on capital improvements.

After five years, their home has increased in value from $175,000 to $242,025 and the Remaining Principal Balance of their loan is $152,743. So their Equity is $89,282. And, like the first scenario, they qualify under Section 121 of the Internal Revenue Code to sell their home and exclude all Capital Gains tax on the profit.

After five years, the numbers for each of the three rental properties is the same.

Each one has increased in value from $165,000 to $228,195 and the Remaining Principal Balance of each loan is $101,867. So, the Equity in each is $125,328. If the properties are sold at this point, it will be necessary for Harold and Mary to do a Section 1031 Exchange in order to avoid taxation on the Capital Gains and the Depreciation Recapture.

But instead of selling, they can free up their Equity with a refinance, and the loan proceeds will not be taxable, and they can continue to operate the rental properties.

So, after five years under this second scenario, Harold and Mary started with $160,000 and now have:

1.) A home with a FMV of $242,025 and with Equity of $89,282 and which will be tax-free if they decide to take out the Equity by selling the property.

2.) Three rental properties each with a FMV of $228,195 for a total of $684,585. Each has Equity of $125,238 for a total of $378,984.

The total Purchase Price of the home and three rental properties was $670,000 and the total FMV today is $926,610.

This represents a Return On Investment (ROI) of 38.3% for five years.

Their total Equity in their home and three rental properties is $468,266.

This represents a Cash On Cash Return (COCR) of 92.67% in five years for their Equity, because they put in $160,000 cash as Equity and now have $468,266 in Equity.

They will also have a COCR for their monthly Cash Flow, which we don't have the number for, but which I explain under Available Resources below.

CONCLUSION

These two examples use a very simplified structure, and there will actually be other factors to consider. But they are chosen to show the value of using your cash efficiently and profitably.

In the first case, buying a home and living in it is a good idea, although maybe not the best idea. It's all about comfort.

Whatever your investment strategy is, it should be one that allows you to sleep well at night.

But a hard fact of life is that you will have to pay, in some manner, for a place to live during your lifetime. If you do not own your own place, you will be paying someone else.

A home of your own eliminates that requirement to pay someone else, every month, for a place to live, as well as just being a good way to invest your money. It's protected in a way that no other investment is protected.

There are also other advantages to investing in your own home.

I explain all of these advantages in my book, "Section 121 Real Estate Investing System," which I strongly recommend that you read, just for the knowledge, even if you don't set up such an investment system.

For example, Harold and Mary did not have to wait five years to sell their home. They could have converted the home into a rental property after **two years, rented it out for three years, and still sold it after five years and excluded all of the Capital Gains tax, using Section 121, even for the Capital Gains that accrued for the three years that the property was used as a rental property.**

No Capital Gains tax on a rental property that they owned for three years!

Meanwhile, they could have bought another property to live in as their principal residence when they sold the first one after two years, and they could have done the same thing with it after **another two years, and at the end of the five year period they could have owned two rental properties as well as a home.**

This is the "system" that I describe in "Section 121 Real Estate Investing System."

And in the second scenario, they could have done the same thing, and after five years they would have ended up with a home and five rental properties, instead of three.

Also in the second scenario, since their financing on the three rental properties would be a commercial loan and would probably contain a balloon payment after five years, meaning a refinance, they could institute a strategy that I have always used, involving a "line of credit" loan.

They could refinance two of the properties.

The Fair Market Value of each one is $228,195. With a 70% loan, they could borrow $159,746. The payoff of the existing Note is $101,867. That leaves $57,870 cash from each refinance of two of the properties. The total is $115,739 in cash.

They use the $115,739 to pay off the debt on the third rental property, so that they now own it free and clear, plus an extra $10,000 cash.

They could use the third rental property as collateral on a "line of credit" loan, and tie it to a draw account.

The way this works is that the Lender authorizes up to $150,000 to be used at any time for any reason without further collateral, and without going through the loan application process. Interest is charged only for the time that a draw has been made until it is paid back.

The interest rate will be the commercial rate, short term, maybe a couple of points higher, but it is well worth it.

They use this as a constant supply of cash that can be used at a moment's notice, for any reason and without qualification. They just call the Lender and have funds put into the account and the money will be there when the check arrives.

I've used such an arrangement to grab some great investments when the owner needed cash immediately, and the other potential buyers were "all hat and no cattle."

In real estate investing, you have to use your own cash wisely, and you have to get into a position where you can qualify for easy access to outside cash with no hassle, and with low cost.

SELECTED RESOURCES

BOOKS

The best real estate investing system I have ever seen involves using your personal residence as a start, and then accumulating virtually unlimited wealth, with no hassle, easy financing, and very predictable results.

I have explained the entire process in my book:

"Section 121 Real Estate Investing System" by Michael Lantrip, available in digital and print at amazon.com/dp/B085LTPK7W.

CALCULATIONS

One of the very best ways to analyze a real estate investment is to determine how much cash you will be getting back, in return for the cash that you invest.

The way to do this is with the Calculation called the Cash On Cash Return, referred to as the COCR.

The following is from my book, "50 Real Estate Investing Calculations." It is available from Amazon.com, and you can go to amazon.com/dp/ B077ZFNZKN and read a few Chapters to see if it would be useful for you.

Or you can go to my website, MichaelLantrip. com, and do the same thing.

Cash On Cash Return

In addition to your COCR for your Equity, you have COCR for your monthly Cash Flow. And you don't have to wait five years to know this number. You can calculate it at any time while you own the property, based on your Cash Flow.

The Cash On Cash Return (COCR) is the relationship between a property's Cash Flow (CF) and the Initial Capital Investment (ICI).

Cash Out versus Cash In.

And we have a Calculation for that.

Cash On Cash Return equals the Cash Flow divided by the Initial Capital Investment.

If it took you $50,000 to get into the property, and it cash flowed you $10,000 the first year, your Cash On Cash Return is 20%.

Let's look at the Calculation.

COCR = CF ÷ ICI, where

COCR is the Cash On Cash Return,

CF is the property's Cash Flow, and

ICI is the Initial Capital Investment required to acquire the property.

To make it easier, let's use a free online Calculator.

https://www.ajdesigner.com/php_cash_on_cash/cash_on_rate.php

1.) For "annual cash flow (ACF)" enter 10000 (no comma).

2.) For "cash invested (CI)" enter 50000.

3.) Click "Calculate."

Your Cash On Cash Return is 20%.

You can also create other Calculations that might be helpful, using this same one, just by rearranging the elements. The ajdesigner.com site has some examples below the Calculation.

But I would ignore their recommendation for a book to read for more information. It is very outdated and not useful.

I have put together all of the Calculations that you will ever need in "50 Real Estate Investing Calculations" which, again, you can find at amazon.com/dp/B077ZFNZKN.

INTERNET

As I said before, Section 121 of the Internal Revenue Code is the most powerful tool that a real estate investor can have.

It is also one of the few sections of the Internal Revenue Code that can be read without special prior knowledge, and can be easily understood. So I have provided a link for you.

Text of Section 121, Internal Revenue Code.

www.law.cornell.edu/uscode/text/26/121

CHAPTER 5

I GUARANTEE IT

OVERVIEW

One person, or one legal entity, can guarantee an obligation of another person or legal entity, and have that guarantee be legally binding.

It's called a Guaranty Agreement.

This is usually done with a written document, and the terms and conditions of the Guaranty Agreement are set out in the document.

In Real Estate Investing, because there is usually a loan involved, this situation comes about when the owner of an LLC agrees to be responsible for the repayment of a loan that is made to that person's LLC.

The loan is usually secured by a lien on the real estate that is owned in the name of the LLC, and the Guaranty Agreement from the owner of the LLC to the Lender is on top of that, to add additional security for the Lender.

The Guaranty Agreement can be a great real estate investing tool for the real estate investor, or it can be a disaster.

It depends on how you go about it.

WHAT HAPPENED

Anthony has wanted to invest in real estate all through school, but he could not.

He was focused on the degree process, and becoming licensed as a Dentist. He knew that he had to spend every minute concentrating on his goal.

But now that he has been in practice about a year, and things are starting to settle down and he can see a fairly comfortable business future, he is thinking again about getting into Real Estate Investing.

He has friends who have done some investing, and a couple of them are looking to go into it full time. He is now considering hooking up with them in some kind of venture.

He knows that he should not do this in his own name, but should use a legal entity.

And he knows that the business entity should be a Limited Liability Company (LLC), in order to protect himself personally from any liability of the LLC, and also in order to protect the LLC and his friends from any personal liability that he might incur in his Dental Practice.

After much discussion and planning, Anthony and three friends formed the Four Amigos LLC and bought a Fourplex to remodel and rent out.

The Fourplex had been neglected, had only three tenants, all of them now on a month-to-month basis, and the rents were low.

The LLC planned to turn it into a quality property and attract longterm tenants at higher rents.

The price of the Fourplex was $540,000 and they would need about $60,000 for the remodeling.

The total would be $600,000 and the Lender was willing to loan the LLC about $480,000 for purchase and renovation if each Member came up with $30,000 to cover the Down Payment of $120,000. The Lender would hold the $60,000 in a Construction Account and disburse it in four draws.

The Lender was willing to make the loan directly to the LLC because the owners were all established businessmen, and the Borrowers were each willing to sign a personal Guaranty on the LLC loan.

They were each a Member Manager of the LLC, and they met once a month to go over the financial aspects of the remodeling, and the renting of the units as they became ready to rent.

They always had a great time, with beer and pizza, and one of the guys, Roger, who was overseeing the work, seemed to have a handle on everything.

Just before they finished with the third unit, Roger spoke up at one of the meetings, and said, "Guys, I think we might have a problem. I'm not sure I can make this month's note payment. One of the tenants is a couple of months delinquent, and the other two rent checks are just not enough. And I am running low on the funds in the remodeling account. We might have to pony up some more funds."

They were not worried and they still believed it was a solid investment. They agreed on how much would be needed from each of them.

The following month, the same thing happened, and Roger said that he just could not handle the situation. "When we started, I didn't know there would be this much bookkeeping and accounting involved."

They agreed to hire an Accountant to get things under control, and each wrote a check to cover his retainer.

The following month, the Accountant attended the meeting, with his report, and told them that the project would not cash flow.

They paid too much. They borrowed too much. They bought more expensive material than they should. They didn't get competitive bids on the work. And their management and rent collection was sloppy.

He told them the exact dollar amount that each would have to contribute each month to break even, at least until the remodeling was completed.

They didn't have a choice, so they agreed to do it.

At the following monthly meeting, the Accountant told them that not everyone was making their contributions, and the Mortgage payment had not been made, and they were running out of remodeling funds.

"I have a copy of the Income Statement and Balance Sheet for each of you," he said. "And I am going to leave now, so that you can discuss the situation."

After much discussion, it turned out that the "situation" was that the investment would not even cash flow enough to make the total note payment each month, and Anthony was the only one of the four with the financial ability to come up with his portion of the negative amount.

Anthony agreed to cover the entire negative for that month, his and the other three, while they tried to find a solution to the problem.

The following monthly meeting was short.

Nothing had changed. And Anthony said he could not continue to cover the negative alone. Nobody offered any solutions, and everybody went home.

The note payment was missed that month, and each of the persons who had signed a Guaranty Agreement received a letter from the Lender requesting the payment.

No one made it.

The Accountant had been given control of the bank account, and, instead of making the Note payment, was using the rent payments to try to pay off the bills from the remodeling so that no liens would be filed on the property, which would cause the Lender to call the Note.

The following month, the Note payment had still not been made and the Lender sent Certified letters to each of the four Guarantors, and also reported the delinquency to the three major Credit Reporting agencies.

That's when it hit the fan.

Years before, when Anthony started his Dental Practice, he had borrowed big-time for the medical building and equipment, and had even gotten his parents to co-sign on the note.

Of course, when his Lender on his business Note was notified by the Credit Reporting agencies that Anthony was in default on another half-million dollar loan, one that they did not even know about, the Lender notified Anthony, and his parents, that he was overextended on his credit limit, and some type of modification of the loan would have to be made, and that they would be operating under a grace period while the situation is dealt with.

The following month, the note on the Fourplex was 90 days delinquent, and the Lender notified the LLC and all of the Guarantors that the note was being Accelerated, the entire amount was being declared Due and Payable, and that they had 30 days to pay it, or the property would be posted for Foreclosure.

The Accountant attended the meeting and told the Members that, in his opinion, a Foreclosure Sale would only bring about 65% of the amount of the Note on the property. He explained that each of the Members, because of the Guaranty that each one signed, was totally responsible for the 35% of the Note that would remain unpaid.

Anthony knew that he was probably the only one with sufficient assets, and, therefore, the one that the Lender would go after first to try to collect the $147,000 Delinquency.

So he proposed to the other Members that they should transfer their ownership interest in the LLC to him, and he would assume the debts, since he was probably the one on which the liabilities would actually fall anyway. He thought that he could pledge the Accounts Receivable of his Dental Practice to the Lender in return for the Lender reinstating the Loan, with modifications, and with payment amounts equal to the Cash Flow available to handle them.

The LLC losses would at least provide some benefit to him, because he could deduct them from the profits from his Dental Practice, which was still doing very well.

The other Members agreed, except for Roger, who said that he had put $30,000 into the investment, and had devoted a lot of time to the project, and did not feel that he should end up with nothing. He insisted on receiving $30,000 for his interest.

Anthony said that in that case, they need to talk about Bankruptcy, but the other Members were unwilling to consider filing Bankruptcy for the LLC.

The group was ultimately unable to work together to deal with the problem.

The Lender filed Foreclosure on the Fourplex.

The Foreclosure Sale brought in enough Net Sale Proceeds to pay $273,000 of the Note, leaving a Delinquency of $147,000.

Anthony received a Notice of Delinquency from the Lender, and a Notice of Intent to Institute Collection for the full amount.

Anthony also received a Notice of Acceleration from the Lender on his Dental Practice note, stating that he was in violation of the Deed of Trust provision that provided that he would not incur any additional liability without prior approval, and that he would do nothing to imperil the security for the loan.

Anthony had no choice but to file Bankruptcy under Chapter 13 and go through a reorganization of his personal and business finances, wiping out the $147,000 liability for the Delinquency from the Foreclosure, and instituting new payment terms on the financing arrangements for the Dental Practice, and imposing those on the Lender. And his parents were required to sign agreements to the entire process.

So, in the end, Anthony lost his $30,000 Down Payment, another $10,000 in contributions to the project, plus another $10,000 in legal fees.

In addition to the $50,000 out-of-pocket, he lost the potential profit from the investment, as well as his relationships with three longtime friends.

His professional reputation also suffered, because people love to gossip.

His Credit Report will show a Foreclosure for the next ten years, at which time it will drop off. But in the meantime, he will be operating under a 3-5 year Bankruptcy Plan.

WHAT SHOULD HAVE HAPPENED

Signing a loan guaranty is actually not a bad idea.

When a Lender is willing to accept a loan guaranty in return for making a large loan to an LLC, when that LLC was just formed and has no credit history, and no income history, you have a very positive situation.

But before you do it, you should understand that there is not just one type of guaranty.

There are actually three types of guaranty:

1.) Loan Guaranty (which is really a "blanket" guaranty).

2.) Backup Guaranty.

3.) Loss Guaranty.

The first one, Loan Guaranty, means a blanket guaranty of the loan. And that, of course, means that you personally guarantee the loan payments.

If a payment is late, or missed, you get a letter, along with the LLC getting the same letter, notifying you of the situation.

This is the same level of responsibility as you would have if you were the Borrower yourself.

This is the type of guaranty that Anthony signed in the previous scenario.

But there were two other types of guaranty available for Anthony.

He could have negotiated the second type of guaranty, the Backup Guaranty.

The Backup Guaranty is a guaranty in which you become the Guarantor if the original Borrower fails to meet its responsibility.

The point at which this failure is considered to have occurred is negotiable between you and the Lender, but the usual timeline of events is that the Lender will proceed all the way to the point of posting the real estate for Foreclosure, and then the Lender notifies you, the Backup Guaranty.

At this point, the Backup Guaranty steps in and pays off the Remaining Principal Balance of the Note, and the Lender transfers the lien on the property to the Backup Guaranty.

If the person who is the Backup Guaranty is the only member of the LLC, what will usually happen is that instead of paying off the Note, the Backup

Guaranty will just re-finance the property with another Lender.

But, if the person who has signed as a Backup Guaranty is just one of the Members of the LLC which has defaulted on the Note, as Anthony would have been in the previous scenario if each Member had signed as a Backup Guaranty, he would offer to release the other Members from their Backup Guaranty in return for their transfer of their interest in the LLC to him, and if they agreed, he would proceed with the re-finance.

But, if the other Backup Guaranties would not agree, then Anthony would need to come up with the funds himself to pay off the Note and get the lien in his name, and then he would have to Foreclose on the LLC.

At the Foreclosure Sale, he would buy the property himself, bidding up to the amount of the Remaining Principal Balance of the Note.

Then he could re-finance the project in his own name or his own LLC.

Then he would be the owner all of the interest in the property.

This is not as cumbersome as it sounds, and I will explain why, when I discuss the Operating Agreement later.

The third type of guaranty is usually called the Loss Guaranty.

In this situation, the Lender Forecloses, sells the property, applies the Net Sales Proceeds to the Remaining Principal Balance of the Note, and then calculates the Deficiency, the amount still owed.

The person who is the Loss Guaranty is then responsible for paying the Deficiency amount to the Lender, but receives nothing in return.

Anthony probably would not have benefited from using this type of guaranty, because in the end, the liability involved for each of the Members who signed the Loss Guaranty is liability called "joint and several," meaning that each one is responsible for the entire amount, not a fractional portion.

And because Anthony is still the one with the most assets, he would still be the first one that the Lender would pursue.

So, what should Anthony have done.

Well, obviously being a Backup Guaranty or a Loss Guaranty would have been better than the blanket Loan Guaranty, but only if Anthony had dealt with the situation in the Operating Agreement that the Members signed when they formed the LLC.

Remember that the LLC, as a business arrangement, is really just a contract by and among the Members.

And the terms of that contract are written in the document called the Operating Agreement.

Every LLC should have an Operating Agreement, but surprisingly, many do not, and usually the situation is that a single Member does not think that he needs an Agreement with himself. And he doesn't, but the Operating Agreement also stands as a statement, and proof, to everyone else, about how the LLC was intended to be operated, in case of disagreement or litigation.

The Operating Agreement will lay out:

1.) Interest ownership of Members.

2.) Rights and responsibilities of Members.

3.) Type of Management.

4.) Allocation of profits.

5.) Manner of holding meetings and voting.

6.) Buyout provisions.

7.) Timeline for profit distributions.

8.) Voting power of Members and Managers.

9.) Limits on disposing of LLC interests.

10.) Member death and disability.

11.) Dispute resolution.

And it can, and probably will, include many other provisions.

For Anthony, the Operating Agreement would have addressed the situation where the Members became liable for personal payment of the Note.

If the Members had signed a blanket Loan Guaranty, the Operating Agreement would have provided that when the obligation kicked in, each Member must make their prorata portion of a Note Payment, and if they failed to do so, their interest in the LLC would be forfeited to the Member or Members who paid their obligation.

If the Members had signed a Backup Guaranty, the Operating Agreement would have provided that when the Foreclosure was posted, and the entire Note had to be paid, the Member who did not pay his share would have his interest in the LLC transferred to the Member or Members who did pay his share.

If the Members had signed a Loss Guaranty, the Operating Agreement would have had no provisions to cover the situation, because when the Loss Guaranty obligation kicked in, the property had already been foreclosed on and the LLC had no interest to transfer from one Member to another.

So, what probably should have happened is that Anthony should have negotiated a Backup Guaranty for the Members, and then have the Operating Agreement include the provisions described above, so that only those Members who participated in paying off the Note would receive the Lien that would then be foreclosed against the LLC.

And this provision could be enforced before the fact of foreclosure, so that those Members who were to receive the Lien could arrange for re-financing prior to having to pay off the Note, instead of having to come up with the funds personally.

CONCLUSION

Participating in an investment with other investors is a very difficult situation, especially when you have a prior relationship with those individuals.

But you should never, under any circumstances, ignore good business practices in the process.

It's true that dealing with such matters in advance might cause the project to never get off the ground, and might also cause some of those relationships to be put under a great deal of strain temporarily.

But failing to deal with such matters will cause an eventual train wreck, and will damage both the investment project and the personal relationships beyond repair and forever.

Signing a personal guaranty can be a great way to handle your real estate investing, and it can also be the worst mistake you every make.

Understand how it works, and deal with it accordingly.

CHAPTER 6

COMBINING AN LLC WITH A PARTNERSHIP

OVERVIEW

The two most popular business setups for real estate investors is the Limited Liability Company (LLC), and the Partnership.

And doing business as a Partnership is usually considered to be a bad idea, because of the lack of control over your personal liability, among other things.

But if you set up the Partnership correctly, it can be a good idea, and maybe a great idea.

For the strongest protection possible against personal liability, you use an LLC.

And you use a Partnership if you want the most flexibility.

But, you can do both at the same time, and get both benefits.

And I'll show you how.

WHAT HAPPENED

Alice and Jane had been good friends since High School.

Now they worked in the same area of town, often had lunch together, and usually talked about their favorite subjects – interior decorating, design, and arts and crafts.

Jane's husband, Bob, had worked for a number of Builders in a variety of construction jobs, and now had his own company doing carpentry, electrical, painting and plumbing work.

Jane had helped Bob with a few of his jobs, mainly picking the colors and making the bathroom and kitchen decisions, with Alice helping them out when she had time. They had always gotten lots of compliments on their choices.

So, one day at lunch, Alice and Jane decided that they should consider starting their own business. They would find rental properties that needed a lot of attention, or distressed properties that could be turned into rental properties.

Their "unique advantage" over their competition would be that they could design and decorate the properties better than, as Alice put it, "Some hairy-legged Gomer with a hammer," which was her perception of most remodelers.

"You mean like my husband," Jane asked?

"No, Bob's alright," Alice said. "At least he knew enough to let you pick the colors and fixtures and materials on his last three projects."

They were certain that their rental properties would be stylish and attractive, and that they would rent faster and stay rented longer. They both loved what Joanna did for Chip (or is Chip working for Joanna?), and they felt that they had the same sense of style.

Alice worked for a local Title Company, so she knew how to use real estate records to find the properties, probably before anyone else knew about them.

And Jane worked in the County Clerk's Office, so she was friends with just about everybody who came in filing documents or otherwise dealing with real estate, and had listened to them talk about what they were doing.

Alice and Jane would keep their jobs, and start the business on the side, and they were pretty sure that Bob would be able to do the actual remodeling work, and would give them a fair bid.

There are no guarantees, and they knew that, but they decided that they would go ahead and set up their business.

They had heard the "rule" that friends should never go into business together, but like everyone else, they hadn't really thought about it, or were sure that it didn't apply to them.

Alice had been involved in a lot of real estate closings for the Title Company, and she knew that the successful investors used a Limited Liability Company (LLC) for protection against personal liability, and that they usually made it a Sub S Corp in order to avoid the 15.3% Self-Employment Taxes.

Jane had seen the same thing in the real estate filings, and they decided that this is the way they would go.

Two days later, Jane called Alice.

"We need to talk," she said.

Over lunch, Jane explained that Bob did not like the idea of her starting a company, and then being an employee, which she would have to do in order to maintain the Sub S status.

And Bob didn't see the need for all of the expense and paperwork of setting up an LLC, since he did not have one for his business, and he had never been sued.

"He's never died either," Alice said. "Does he think that means that he won't?"

"Hey, I'm with you," Jane said. "But what can I do? You're not married, you don't know how these things work. Besides, I think that he feels that if we <u>don't</u> do the LLC, and you and I operate as partners, then he owns part of my part. I don't know."

Alice and Jane had been friends for a long time, and they really wanted to do this, and they were not going to let it go.

So they set up business as a General Partnership.

Jane found copies of some partnership agreements that had been filed in the public records, and they just copied one of those.

They found a property that was structurally sound, didn't need a lot of work but was totally outdated, for $50,000.

They thought that they could maintain its "Craftsman" charm without changing very much, but totally redecorate and update the appliances and fixtures, for about $20,000.

The labor would run another $10,000 but Bob had agreed to wait until the project was finished, leased, and refinanced to be paid.

They got a bank loan for $40,000 to purchase the property, each coming up with $6,000 to cover the Down Payment and Closing Costs.

They planned to use credit cards to cover the remodeling costs.

At first, it was nothing but fun.

They loved tearing out old, ugly stuff.

And they didn't understand what they were seeing underneath, until Bob came in and saw the problems. The foundation was still level, but the termites had eaten all they wanted and left. The piers and beams were in that certain condition that they are in just before they collapse. Many of the piers and beams would have to be replaced, and more needed to be added just to be safe, and that meant tearing out all of the floors.

This would add to their material and labor cost, which would probably eat up most of the profit that they hoped to make, and would probably delay some of the work, since Bob would be doing work that he would not be paid for until the end of the project, and he needed to do other things in the meantime to make a living at the same time.

Although Bob was the one who failed to detect the true extent of the problem in the initial inspection, they didn't say so, because they appreciated him being willing to work for them and delay being paid.

They thought that they were dealing well with the problem.

But then, the real problem happened.

While the floors were out, and it was not possible to secure the property, some kids from the neighborhood came onto the property and were playing inside the house, when one of them fell through the opening, and was severely injured.

The lawsuit was filed, the Homeowner's Insurance Policy agreed to settle for their limits of $50,000 but the total possible from a court verdict was in the hundreds of thousands.

Alice and Jane did not have the funds to even hire a Lawyer, even though they talked to a couple who were friends, and were told that they really had no defense, and were likely to have a large judgment entered.

They could not afford to defend the lawsuit, and a Default Judgment was entered against them. Since the State in which they lived was a Community Property State, Bob was included in the ownership of the property and was included in the Judgment.

In order to save what assets they could, they both had to file for Bankruptcy protection.

The whole process took about two years.

They lost their dream. They lost their public reputation. They saw less and less of each other. Jane and Bob moved away, and later got a divorce.

Of course, the Lender foreclosed on the property, and served them with Notice of Deficiency since the Net Sales Proceeds from the Foreclosure did not pay off the Note, but the Deficiency was wiped out with the Bankruptcy.

The only money lost was the Down Payment, the amount of the materials that they had charged on their credit cards, and the work that Bob had done and not been paid for.

It all happened because in a General Partnership, each Partner has unlimited liability for all of the debts and obligations of the Partnership, and the Partner's own assets can be taken to satisfy those obligations.

WHAT SHOULD HAVE HAPPENED

When Jane told Alice that their plan to set up as an LLC was not going to happen, because her husband, Bob, thought that they should just be 50-50 partners, and he also did not see any need to incur the expenses of an LLC, they went to a Lawyer who practiced primarily in the area of Business Law.

He also practiced Real Estate Law and Tax Law, but the focus of the visit was the structure of the anticipated business venture.

He explained to them how they could be LLCs and still operate as a Partnership.

Alice created her entity, "AliceLand, LLC" and filed Form 8832 electing to be treated as a Sub S Corp for tax purposes.

Jane's husband refused to go to the expense of creating an LLC, but Alice said that in order to add to her own personal protection, and because she was a friend in addition to a business associate, that she would pay the cost of the "JB, LLC" for Jane and Bob. They did not file Form 8832 and therefore chose to have their LLC be treated for tax purposes as a Disregarded Entity, which means that they would report everything on their personal tax return, just as though the property were in their name.

The two LLCs then entered into a Partnership Agreement.

The property would be owned jointly by the two LLCs and they would have equal voice in everything. They included a Buy-Sell Provision to cover the eventuality of a conflict.

Since it would be difficult to get financing for two new LLCs, they went to a Hard Money Lender, Clark HML.

They took all of their paperwork for the LLCs, all of the documents relating to the property, and their materials and labor list.

They had a real estate agent give them an estimate of the After-Repair Value (ARV) of $120,000.

Clark reviewed all of the documentation, inspected the property, and agreed to make a 55% loan on the project, a total of $66,000.

The interest rate would be 10% for 6 months, an APR of 20%.

Clark required that the LLCs put up $10,000 as part of the Purchase Price of the property, and another $2,000 to cover Closing Costs.

Clark would pay the remaining $40,000 of the Purchase Price, and hold the $26,000 for construction, and would disburse it in draws, although only $20,000 was anticipated as being needed.

"It doesn't hurt to have an extra $6,000 in reserve. That way, if the need comes up, we don't have to re-do the documents."

When the foundation problem was discovered, they didn't panic.

They called Clark HML, who came out and looked at the problem, and agreed to change and initial the materials and labor list, and said that if the $6,000 reserve amount did not cover it, Jane and Alice would just have to buy some of the other materials, like paint, on their personal credit cards.

Then tragedy struck, and a neighborhood child was injured on the property.

Although they could have claimed that they had done everything reasonable to secure the site from intruders, most court cases have found that, in the case of children, almost everything qualifies as an "attractive nuisance," and that establishes liability for any injuries.

However, there were other things that caused them to not give up.

They did have a Homeowner's Insurance Policy that had a provision that could cover payment for such claims, but it was not entirely clear.

Also, if a lawsuit was filed, it would have to be against the LLCs, and the only asset available to satisfy a Judgment resulting from such a lawsuit would be the real estate. And the value of the real estate in its current condition, after everything had been ripped out of it, including the floors, was even less than when it was purchased for $50,000, probably about $35,000. And if the real estate was taken, it would have to be taken with the debt against it, which was $66,000.

So the Lawyer representing the injured child agreed with the LLCs to release them from liability in return for the proceeds from the Homeowner's Policy, which was eventually negotiated to be the maximum of $50,000.

With the threat of a lawsuit gone, Alice and Jane completed the remodeling of the real estate within six months, and sold it for $120,000 to a retired Teacher, who absolutely loved the design and decoration.

They had originally planned to make this the first rental property in their Portfolio, but they decided that they needed to put this one behind them, and start again with a new perspective.

The Loan Payoff was $66,000 in Principal and $6,600 in Interest, for a total of $72,600. Closing Costs were another $1,200.

Bob was paid $12,200 for all of the work he had done.

Their Net Sales Proceeds from the Closing was $34,000.

They set up an Educational Trust Fund for the injured child with $14,000.

They took the other $20,000 and went to lunch to plan their next project.

CONCLUSION

The biggest mistake made by Real Estate Investors is not using a business entity.

The second biggest mistake is using the wrong one.

SELECTED RESOURCES

FREE BOOK CHAPTER

In Chapter 3, "Me Or LLC," I included a Chapter about the LLC from my book, "Your Best Business Entity For Real Estate Investing."

I urge you to read that if you have not done so.

Now, I will provide you a Chapter from the same book about the General Partnership.

You will notice that both Chapters are laid out the same, with the same Sections in each, so that you can do a direct comparison of the elements and characteristics of each entity between Chapters.

CHAPTER 5

GENERAL PARTNERSHIP

OVERVIEW

A General Partnership is like a Sole Proprietorship, except that it involves more than one person.

A General Partnership is automatically created when two or more persons start a business.

We will refer to "two" so as to keep it simple and understandable.

But there will be no systemic differences between two and more than two.

A General Partnership can also be an association of two legal entities that are not individuals.

For Example, two LLCs can enter into a General Partnership arrangement.

If they do, this will create a stacked entity arrangement in which the main activity is being conducted as a Partnership, and then the Partners are operating as a different entity.

For Example, one of the LLCs can be a Single Member LLC that has elected to be treated as a Disregarded Entity for tax purposes, and the other LLC can be a Single Member LLC that has elected to be treated as an S Corp for tax purposes.

Or, the second LLC can be a Multi Member LLC that has elected to be treated as a Partnership for tax purposes.

The General Partnership arrangement can be just the final way in which the Entities have decided to set things up.

So, it is not always true that you should never operate as a General Partnership.

FORMATION

There is no formality, or legal procedure, required to form a General Partnership.

It can be done just by two persons starting a business, or investing in property.

However, this is a very, very bad way to do it.

The majority of business disputes that I have seen in the past forty years involved two persons who suddenly claimed to have different understandings concerning their business arrangement.

The correct way to form a General Partnership is to create a General Partnership Agreement.

The Agreement will state the terms of the business arrangement and how the Partnership will be formed, operated, and dissolved.

It will cover such matters as:

1.) Initial Capital Contribution.

2.) Ownership Percentage.

3.) Profit and Loss Allocation.

4.) Division of tasks and responsibilities.

5.) Management.

6.) Dispute resolution.

7.) Dissolution and distribution of assets.

You might be required to file or register your Partnership with the State, depending on where you live.

You will also need to file an Assumed Name Certificate, or whatever is required in the jurisdiction in which you live.

Your Partnership must have a name, such as ABC Partnership.

The Assumed Name Certificate which you file in the county records will identify the Partnership, the Partners, and the address of the business, as well as any other required information.

And finally, you will need to obtain an Employer Identification Number (EIN) from the IRS.

FINANCING

A General Partnership is a legal entity and can enter into a loan agreement with a Lender in order to obtain financing.

The debt will be secured by the assets of the General Partnership, and the Lender will probably require an additional Guarantee from such of the Partners who have the credit to satisfy the Lender.

The ownership of the General Partnership will generally follow the amount of the capital contributions.

If Bob puts in $100,000 and John and Mary each put in $50,000, then Bob will own 50% of the General Partnership, and John and Mary will each own 25%.

The Partners are also allowed to contribute property in return for ownership interest in the General Partnership.

This will not usually be a taxable event, but it will require careful accounting of the Partners Capital Accounts to make sure that all rules of the IRS are followed.

Contributing property with debt is particularly tricky and will require some complicated calculations by an accountant.

MANAGEMENT

If there is no written agreement, a General Partnership is managed by all of the Partners.

If there is a written agreement, the management will be stipulated in the written agreement.

If there are more than a few Partners, or most do not have the time to take part, the written agreement will designate one person as the Managing Partner.

The IRS will require a declaration of who will be the Tax Partner, and this is a very important decision for everyone. The Tax Partner is authorized to deal with the IRS on behalf of the Partnership.

For the person agreeing to be the Tax Partner, it entails a lot of responsibility, and some liability.

For the rest of the Partners, it could mean turning over the right to make decisions affecting the General Partnership and the other Partners without consultation, and without recourse.

Be very careful with the Tax Partner designation.

OPERATING THE BUSINESS

A written partnership agreement will stipulate the manner in which the General Partnership will be managed.

You are free to write the Partnership Agreement to include any provisions, but be aware that the general public is entitled to accept the statements and behavior of any Partner as representing the entire General Partnership, and any Partner can create binding obligations and liability.

The actions of any Partner that result in a claim or lawsuit can also cause those actions to be taken against the General Partnership.

It is critical to have very strict control measures in place for a General Partnership.

BUYING REAL ESTATE

The real estate can be purchased in the name of the General Partnership, but if there is no written agreement that outlines the terms of the purchase, management, and eventual sale of the property, it can lead to the real estate being locked into a contested ownership situation and might cause the real estate to become unmarketable.

It is usually best to own the real estate in the name of the General Partnership, but it is critical that this subject be thoroughly detailed in the Partnership Agreement.

And if Partners are required by the Lender to stand behind any financing, it is always better for the Guaranty used to be one in which the Partners are only responsible for any loss the Lender may suffer if it becomes necessary to foreclose on the real estate and sell it to recover the loan proceeds.

The other Guaranty is one where the Partners become immediately responsible if the Lender sends a notice of default or delinquency, and this should be avoided if possible.

CONTRIBUTING OWNED REAL ESTATE

Contributing real estate to a General Partnership in return for Partnership Interest is a possible way of funding the enterprise.

But the possible complications are too numerous to go into here, and would require discussing your particular situation with an accountant who is very knowledgeable about partnership accounting.

And there are many other ways of arriving at the same situation without this complication.

As an Example, you might create an LLC and contribute your real estate to the Single Member LLC in return for all of the Capital Interest. And then your LLC can lease the real estate to the General Partnership, and the General Partnership will function basically as an operating company with limited ownership of assets.

SELLING REAL ESTATE

If the real estate is owned by the General Partnership, then the General Partnership will be the Seller of the real estate.

It will be done in the manner provided for in the Partnership Agreement.

Selling the real estate just has the effect of turning one Partnership asset, real estate, into another Partnership asset, cash.

So the Net Sales Proceeds of the transaction will be owned by the Partners in the same proportion that the real estate was owned by the General Partnership.

The profit from the sale will be Capital Gains, and will be reported to the Partners on their individual Schedule K-1 (1065) from the annual tax return filed by the General Partnership, the Form 1065, U.S. Return of Partnership Income.

Part of the Capital Gains will be taxed at a different rate, 25%, because it will represent Depreciation Recapture for the depreciation taken on the property while it was being used as rental real estate.

PROVIDING SERVICES

If the General Partnership is engaged in rental

real estate activities, the income created will be passive income.

There will be no Self-Employment (SE) Tax assessed on it, so you do not have to be concerned about dealing with how you provide services to the Partnership.

If you run the rental activities, your compensation will be the income earned by the business.

You can provide as much, or as little, personal service as you wish.

It will not make the income self-employment income, and you will not have to pay the 15.3% SE tax.

That's the good news.

The bad news is that it will still be passive income, and any losses cannot be deducted from your other ordinary income, only from other passive income.

BOOKKEEPING

Partnership Accounting is a special area of Accounting, and is also one of the more difficult areas of Accounting.

Not only must you keep track of the Income and Expenses of the Partnership, but you must also keep track of each Partner's Distributive Share Items.

These include:

1.) Income/Loss.

2.) Deductions.

3.) Self-Employment Earnings.

4.) Credits.

5.) Foreign Transactions.

6.) Alternative Minimum Tax (AMT) Items.

7.) Other Information, such as investment income, tax-exempt interest, etc.

Then you must keep track of each Partner's Capital Account.

The cost of Accounting, and the cost of preparing Tax Returns and Schedules for the Partnership and for the Partners are two of the reasons for not choosing the Partnership as your business entity.

On the other hand, there are so many things you can do with the Partnership business entity structure, it offers more opportunities some of the others.

LIABILITY

A General Partnership has no limit on liability.

All of its assets are subject to the debts of the Partnership.

In addition, each Partner has unlimited liability for all of the Partnership obligations.

If that Partner is an individual, then that liability can spread to all of the individual's personal assets, and even business assets if they are not protected inside a Business Entity.

If the Partner is an LLC, then the LLC still has unlimited liability for all of the Partnership obligations, but that liability does not extend to the Owner or Owners of the LLC, who are protected from the liabilities of the LLC.

ENTITY

The General Partnership is a legal entity and can be sued in its own capacity.

The General Partnership has unlimited liability for all of its own activities, and in most cases, the activities of the individual Partners if those activities are associated with the General Partnership.

INDIVIDUAL

For the individual, it is one step farther than when you are a Sole Proprietor and responsible for the debts you create in your company.

In the General Partnership, you are also responsible for debts created by another Partner.

In addition, if the actions of another Partner result in a lawsuit that leads to a Judgment against the General Partnership, you are also responsible for that, even if you did not know about it.

This is because each Partner is an agent of the General Partnership with full authority to bind the General Partnership, and thereby, bind the other Partners, provided that the Partner was acting within the scope of the General Partnership's normal business.

TAXATION

A General Partnership does not pay federal income taxes.

But the Partners do.

So, the General Partnership must file a federal income tax form that shows the IRS the amount of income, expenses, deductions, credits, and other items, for both the Partnership and for the Partners.

It is a Form 1065, U.S. Return of Partnership Income.

The General Partnership is a Pass-Through Entity (PTE), so all of the income, deductions, credits, and other items will pass through to the Partners.

In the States that have an income tax, the form for reporting the State income will be whatever your State requires.

FEDERAL

The required tax form for paying federal taxes is

the Form 1065, U.S. Return of Partnership Income.

But the General Partnership does not pay taxes.

So, the Form 1065 will report the income, expenses, deductions and credits.

Form 1065 contains a schedule called Schedule K.

Schedule K will identify the different types of income, and any credits and deductions that are not deductible at the Partnership level.

The preparer of the Form 1065 will also prepare a Schedule K-1 for each of the Partners, based on the Schedule K.

The Schedule K-1 will allocate the appropriate amounts of income, credits and deductions for each of the Partners.

A copy of the Form 1065, including Schedule K, and all of the K-1s, is sent to the IRS.

Partners will receive a copy of their K-1 for use in preparing their personal tax returns.

You can obtain a copy for the Form 1065 at:

Irs.gov/pub/irs-pdf/f1065.pdf.

You can obtain a copy of the Schedule K-1 at:

Irs.gov/pub/irs-pdf/f1065sk1.pdf.

ENTITY

The reason that the General Partnership does not pay taxes is because it is what is referred to as a "Pass-Through Entity," or PTE.

That means that all of the income, credits and deductions are passed through to the Partners, who report the appropriate amounts on their personal tax returns.

The new 20% Income Exclusion for Qualified Business Income (QBI) of Pass-Through Entities is not deducted at the Partnership level.

Only the individual Taxpayer can claim this exclusion, and the exclusion will be calculated based on the total of that individual's PTE income.

INDIVIDUAL

The individual Taxpayer, the Partner, will receive a Schedule K-1 that contains information about the Partnership and information about the Partner.

When you receive your Schedule K-1 (Form 1065) it will contain all of the information regarding your share of the Partnership's income/loss, deductions, credits, and other items.

It will include amounts for:

1.) Ordinary business income/loss.

2.) Net rental real estate income/loss.

3.) Other net rental income/loss.

4.) Guaranteed payments.

5.) Interest income.

6a.) Ordinary dividends.

6b.) Qualified dividends.

7.) Royalties.

8.) Net short-term capital gains/loss.

9a.) Net long-term capital gains/loss.

9b.) Collectibles (28%) gains/loss.

9c.) Depreciation Recapture.

10.) Net business asset sale gain/loss.

11.) Other income/loss.

12.) Section 179 deduction.

13.) Other deductions.

14.) Self-employment earnings/loss.

15.) Credits.

16.) Foreign transactions.

17.) Alternative Minimum Tax (AMT) items.

18.) Tax-exempt income and nondeductible

expenses.

19.) Distributions.

20.) Other information.

Included with the Schedule K-1 will be extensive directions on exactly where you should put each of the numbers from the K-1 onto your personal tax return.

You will be taxed on these items whether or not you receive the income from the Partnership in the form of a distribution.

The income is added to your Partner Capital Account, and the distributions to you are subtracted from your Partner Capital Account. The balance in your Partner Capital Account is called you "tax basis."

As long as you report your K-1 income on your personal tax return, and as long as your Partner Capital Account balance does not go negative, your distributions themselves are not taxable.

STATE

There are seven States which have no State Income Tax.

They are:

1.) Alaska,

2.) Florida,

3.) Nevada,

4.) South Dakota,

5.) Texas,

6.) Washington, and

7.) Wyoming.

The other States impose some type of tax on income.

The tax rates vary, and the exceptions, exemptions, and thresholds vary.

ENTITY

To determine how your State treats General Partnership, you should access your State's website and read about taxation of Entities.

The situation is different for every State.

INDIVIDUAL

To determine how your State treats Schedule K-1 items, you should access your State's website and read about taxation.

The situation is different for every State.

CONCLUSION

General Partnerships, with individuals as the Partners, are almost never a good idea.

However, the General Partnership is a clean and simple way to structure some businesses, if you take the precautions to limit the liability of each of the participants. It is not unusual for a General Partnership to be formed by a couple of LLCs.

One reason for this would be that the LLCs already have their own liability, but limit the liability for the Owners, and so the unlimited liability of the General Partnership is not a concern.

Another reason would be that one of the two individuals creating the LLCs wants to be taxed as a Disregarded Entity and the other individual creating the other LLC wants to be taxed as an S Corp.

If they just created a Multi Member LLC, they would both be relegated to Partnership as a default taxation, and if they elected a different one, it would have to be the same for both.

But in most situations, two LLCs would not form a General Partnership.

Given the circumstances, the two individuals would each form their own LLC so that they could each choose their own form of taxation, and then the two LLC would create another LLC together instead of joining into a General Partnership arrangement.

General Partnerships have their uses, but with the flexibility of the LLC, and the special tax features of the S Corp, the General Partnership is not very popular anymore.

BOOK CHAPTER REFERENCE TO HML

Hard Money Lending (HML) is a major part of the Real Estate Investing environment today, and if you don't have clear understanding of it, you should do some reading.

Most of what you find on the Blogs and Podcasts will be fragmented, vague, or just not true.

I recommend Chapter 1 in my book "10 Other Real Estate Investment You Could Do" in which I discuss HML from the standpoint of operating a business as a Hard Money Lender. But the information will be what you need to know as a Borrower, as well.

I wanted to include all of it here, but it is 37 pages, and there just was not room.

CHAPTER 7

BUT I DON'T OWN THAT!

OVERVIEW

The protection against personal liability that is provided by certain business entities, in this case an LLC, also comes with certain responsibilities.

In a sense, the protection against personal liability is really "conditional" protection against liability, in the sense that there are conditions that you must meet, and which you must also maintain.

At one time (think bell bottoms), it was necessary to go to an Attorney, or in some cases a CPA, to have a business entity set up for you.

When you did so, they spent most of the time explaining what you should do <u>after</u> the business entity is created, because they were concerned that you should understand how important it is.

Now, with the internet offering everything, and with politicians with no real business knowledge passing laws, you can set up your own business entity by just checking boxes, and you really don't have to know anything about the business entity or how it should be run, to just check boxes.

And, therefore, most people don't know.

Well, hopefully, at this point, you have not suffered, and hopefully this Chapter will provide you with at least some useful information regarding the creating and the dissolving of an LLC.

WHAT HAPPENED

This scenario is a continuation of the story of Alice and Jane, from the previous Chapter 6, "Combining An LLC With A Partnership," and assumes that they did "What Should Have Happened" in that Chapter.

After the success of the first investment, Bob saw the benefit of personal liability protection provided by an LLC, and he decided that he wanted to create one for his construction business.

But Jane said, "Then we would have two LLCs. Do we really need two?"

And Bob said, "Maybe you're right. We would actually just be working together, the two of us. What if we just dissolve JB, LLC since we're finished with this project, and create another LLC. That way, we could elect Sub S Corp status, like you wanted to, and we could pay ourselves salaries, and I could stop paying all of that 15.3% Self-Employment Tax on all of my profits."

Jane agreed, but wondered if it would affect the Partnership Agreement that their LLC had with Alice's LLC. So she called Alice.

"How odd," said Alice, "I have just been thinking that I should really have two separate LLCs, one LLC for decorating and design, and another one strictly for real estate. So I could put AliceLand, LLC on the shelf in case I get any jobs for decorating, and do a new LLC for real estate, call it "Alice Tomorrow, LLC," and then we could do a new Partnership Agreement for our LLCs. We would probably need a new one anyway, one that stipulates that we are each also involved in other activities."

So Alice created a new entity, Alice Tomorrow, LLC, and Jane and Bob created JBob, LLC, and dissolved JB, LLC.

Then they drafted a new Partnership Agreement between Alice Tomorrow, LLC and JBob, LLC.

Over the next couple of years, they bought and renovated three properties, all of which were now producing very good income.

Then Alice received a letter from a Lawyer notifying her that he represented the retired Teacher who had bought the "Craftsman Cottage," and that she had been diagnosed with cancer.

The Lawyer also said that his investigation indicated that the cause was probably old asbestos insulation that had not been removed from the property.

He said that because AliceLand, LLC was one of the sellers of the property, Alice should consult her Lawyer and get back in touch with him.

Jane and Bob had received an identical letter.

Alice immediately took the matter to a Lawyer, who responded to the letter with sympathy and regret, but pointed out that AliceLand, LLC was a dormant business entity that had not been active for two years, that it had no assets and no income, and was therefore effectively "judgment-proof."

When Jane and Bob took their letter to a Lawyer, the situation was quite different.

"So, was JB, LLC one of the sellers of the real estate that we are talking about," the Lawyer asked.

"Yes," said Bob. "But we have no liability, because we were never owners of the property personally, the LLC owned the property, and besides, we've dissolved that LLC."

"Well," said the Lawyer, "let me decide the liability question after I have the full picture. Did you dissolve the LLC by sending in the dissolution forms to the State?"

Bob said that they did, and they had copies to prove it.

The Lawyer explained to Bob and Jane what they had actually done, in terms of the personal liability question.

When you have formed and operated a business entity, such as an LLC, that LLC acquires assets and liabilities. They belong to the LLC. They are the assets of the LLC. And they are the liabilities of the LLC.

When you dissolve a business entity, you distribute the assets and liabilities of the business entity to the owners of the business entity.

"When you dissolved the LLC, did you distribute the assets," the Lawyer asked?

"Well, yes," Bob said. "There was some money in the checking account and we took that when we closed the account. And I had bought some tools, and I have those."

"Were there any liabilities?"

"No, we paid all of the bills before we dissolved the company."

The Lawyer explained that what they had actually done is dissolve the LLC, distribute the assets and the liabilities to the owners, which was themselves, and cease to operate as an LLC.

"So we have no responsibility since the LLC no longer exists, right?"

"No," said the Lawyer, "on the contrary, you have all of the liability that the LLC had because you dissolved the LLC and distributed the liability to yourselves, along with the assets. And liability includes known and unknown. So if this claim is valid, and the LLC would be liable, if the LLC still existed, then you are now liable for it."

"So what do we do," Jane asked, "can you handle this?"

"No," the Lawyer said. "Asbestos litigation is very complex, and defending a case can cost hundreds of thousands of dollars, and can take a lot of time. You might just want to allow a Default Judgment, and wipe it out with personal Bankruptcy to protect the rest of your assets. At least, your real estate and your business is held in the name of your other LLC instead of your own name, so that can't be taken."

WHAT SHOULD HAVE HAPPENED

At the time that Alice and Jane decided that they should change the structure of their business arrangement, they should have gone to a Business Lawyer.

And, as I said before, it should be a Business Lawyer who is also active in the areas of Real Estate Law and Tax Law.

They should have explained to the Lawyer everything that they thought they should do, and then asked the Lawyer what they needed to do from a legal standpoint.

The Lawyer would probably have agreed to the general plan for Alice, and probably would have agreed to what Jane had in mind, except for what they planned to do regarding the two original LLCs.

He would have explained the danger of dissolving an LLC and assuming all of the potential liability that might be asserted against it in the future.

He probably would have advised just having the two LLCs go dormant, and refrain from all activity for a reasonable period of time, with the goal of extinguishing all of the time periods in which anyone might be able to exert a claim against the LLC.

This time period is called "the Statute of Limitations" and is quite complicated, and somewhat complex, but basically it ranges from two years (rare) up to six years (usually the maximum).

But it is still very uncertain, because there is always an argument as to when the time period starts to run. It is not usually when the alleged act that is complained of took place, or when the person suffered from the alleged act, but when the person knew that they had an injury, and a right to sue because of it, called the "accrual of the cause of action."

And this date is the date on which the individual "knew or reasonably should have known" that they had a right to bring a lawsuit. From that point, the Statute of Limitations begins to run.

So, in some way, Alice did "what should have happened" by creating a new LLC after the first project, and so did Jane, although not with the knowledge that it would protect them in the future.

If they had continued using the same two LLCs for the next three projects, the new lawsuit would have been filed against those two original LLCs, and, if successful, all of the assets of the two LLCs, the three rental properties that they now own, would have been taken.

CONCLUSION

Unfortunately, too many real estate investors make their own decisions, usually business decisions, without first getting expert advice.

Sometimes, a business decision is really a legal decision.

And that usually means that you cannot simply apply common sense and business knowledge to it and come up with the right answer.

If it is a legal decision, it depends on two factors that are usually not controlled by common sense and reasoning.

Those two factors are the laws of the State, and the decisions handed down by the Appellate Courts that interpret the meaning of the laws.

And even a Lawyer will usually have to spend a few hours doing legal research before he can confidently advise you on the proper course of action, even when he already knows the area of law.

A half-hour consultation with a Lawyer can turn out to be the best investment you ever made.

SELECTED RESOURCES

LLC INFORMATION

In the Selected Resources section of Chapter 3, "Me Or LLC?" I have included an entire Chapter about the Limited Liability Company from my book "Your Best Business Entity For Real Estate Investing."

I urge you to go there and read that.

PARTNERSHIP INFORMATION

In the Selected Resources section of the prior Chapter, I included an entire Chapter on General Partnerships from my book "Your Best Business Entity For Real Estate Investing."

I urge you to go there and read that.

CHAPTER 8

SELL WITH SELLER FINANCING

OVERVIEW

Some people own Rental Property that is completely paid off.

No debt.

Not many people do, but some do.

And this is a situation that presents an interesting opportunity when it is time to sell the property.

This might even work for you if your property isn't paid off, and just has a low amount of debt.

I've often been asked by Property Owners if they should take out a Mortgage first, and then sell the property.

They are thinking that when the debt on the property, the Mortgage that they just took out, is paid off, that it might reduce the amount of Capital Gains, and therefore the amount of their taxes.

Well, it will not.

Debt payoff is not part of the Capital Gains Calculation.

But hold on.

Strangely, there is actually an advantage to be gained by adding debt to your property before selling it, if you do it in a certain way.

Let's look at a couple of scenarios.

WHAT HAPPENED

Roger was just your average Real Estate Investor.

He worked as an Accountant for a few years. And during this time, as he was establishing his credit, he was also trying to save enough for a decent Down Payment on a property, while looking for his ideal investment.

He liked Duplexes.

Meantime, unexpectedly, he received a cash inheritance of $240,000 on the death of his mother.

Shortly after that, he found his ideal investment property.

That was five years ago.

He bought a Duplex for $300,000 and was able to pay cash because he had it, and the cash wasn't earning anything in the bank.

He had originally intended to live in one side of the Duplex and rent out the other side, but instead, he kept both tenants, and instead, he moved into the house that his mother had left him.

He expected the Duplex to provide good cash flow and good income, which it generally has.

But it has not provided very good capital appreciation, as Roger discovered when he received an offer for $375,000 for the Duplex.

He was not looking to sell, but he was curious, and he checked around and found $375,000 to be fairly representative for similar properties in that area.

It represented slightly less than 5% annual appreciation, and he had expected more, about 7%.

So, after some deliberation, he decided it was time to sell, and find a better investment.

Roger has claimed $50,000 in Depreciation on the property in the five years, so his Adjusted Basis in the property is $250,000.

When he sells, he will have $125,000 of Capital Gains.

This number is the $375,000 Sales Price (and we are ignoring transaction costs for the sake of simplicity) minus the $250,000 Adjusted Basis in the property.

The Capital Gains Tax brackets are 0%, 15%, and 20%.

Roger has a good income, and he is in the 15% Capital Gains Tax bracket.

Of course, $50,000 of the $125,000 of Capital Gains was the result of the $50,000 of Depreciation that he claimed on the property.

It lowered the Adjusted Basis, which increased the calculated Capital Gains.

This $50,000 will be classified as "Depreciation Recapture" instead of Capital Gains, and will be taxed as Ordinary Income, up to a maximum of 25%.

We will assume 25%. And the IRS wants the Depreciation Recapture Tax paid first, before the regular Capital Gains Tax is paid.

The Depreciation Recapture Tax amount will be $12,500.

Now Roger must pay 15% Capital Gains tax on the remaining $75,000 of Capital Gains calculation.

This tax amount will be $11,250.

The total of the two taxes will be $23,750.

After this total tax liability is deducted from the $375,000 Net Sales Proceeds, Roger's after-tax profit is $51,250 on his $300,000 original cash investment five years ago.

This is a little less than 3.5% per year.

Not good.

Of course, he had the monthly income, and assuming that he cleared at least $1,250 per month from the rental activity business, that would have been about 5% annual return.

In any event, after five years, Roger has his $300,000 back, plus $51,250 in profit, and is ready to look for another investment property.

Hopefully, he has now read Chapter 4 about leverage, "Spend Cash, Don't Spend Cash."

WHAT SHOULD HAVE HAPPENED

You have no control over what might happen if you buy into a neighborhood that is on the downside of its life cycle.

There is nothing you can do about it.

It just might happen that a new upscale 200-unit Apartment Complex was just built, and is closer to the University, closer to the new shopping areas, and closer to the restaurants.

There's still nothing wrong with your property.

But the market shifted on you.

You can't control that.

But you can always control your personal finances, and how you manage them.

And what Roger should have done, and maybe what he actually did, if he is a really good Accountant, is take a fresh look at the process of selling real estate, do a little research, and buy this book.

Instead of an outright sale, he found an alternative way to sell the property.

It involves the use of three things:

1.) debt,

2.) an Installment Sale, and

3.) a Wraparound Note.

The first thing Roger did was to take out a 70% loan on the property, at 5%, for 25 years, with a monthly payment of $1,534.55.

This provided him with immediate cash in the amount of $262,500.

This money is tax-free, because it is a loan.

The second thing that he did was sell the property for $375,000 and receive a 30% Down Payment of $112,500.

He did Seller Financing on the Balance with a Wraparound Mortgage for $262,500 at 7% for 25 years, with a monthly payment of $1,855.30.

The Wraparound Note is secured by a lien on the property until the note is paid.

Now, let's look at what Roger has at this point.

1.) $262,500 cash from the underlying loan proceeds.

2.) $112,500 cash from the Down Payment from the Buyer on the Wraparound Note.

3.) a Note Receivable for $262,500 from the Buyer, secured by a $375,000 Duplex.

4.) $1,855.30 in monthly Note payments.

5.) no management responsibility.

6.) no monthly expenses for anything – repairs, taxes, insurance.

7.) monthly cash flow of $320.75 for the next 25 years.

That's hard to imagine.

Let me repeat it.

Roger started the selling process with a Duplex worth $375,000, which he owned free and clear.

Now, he has $375,000 in cash, a Note Receivable for $262,500 secured by a lien on the real estate, a monthly cash flow of $320.75 for 25 years, which is a total of 300 payments, for a total of another $96,225.

His debt on the property will be paid off with the payments from the Wraparound Note he received when he sold the property.

And the property that he sold "subject-to" still has $112,500 in Equity for him, since he only borrowed $262,500 on it, and which is increasing every month, in case the Buyer defaults and Roger has to take the property back.

And to top it all off, he now has no management responsibility and no monthly expenses.

Of course, no situation is perfect, including this one, and there are other factors that Roger must consider.

As you are aware, every Mortgage or Deed of Trust might have a "due on sale" clause in it, and that would make the underlying loan due and payable when the property is sold.

Or it might not have such a clause.

The Lender might be one who enforces such clauses, or the Lender might be happy to just keep the loan on the books as long as the monthly payments are coming in, since the Lender will always have a First Lien on the property securing the original debt.

But Roger must look at the facts of his situation, and consider the situation very seriously, and make his best decision.

He might have to establish an Escrow Account large enough to cover six or twelve months of payments in order to make the Lender comfortable with the situation. Even with that, he is still way ahead.

The other contingency that Roger must deal with is the possibility that the Buyer might refinance at some point, or otherwise come up with the cash, and pay off the $262,500 due on the Wrap-around Note.

In that event, Roger will have to pay off the underlying loan.

No problem.

The Buyer pays Roger the $262,500 and Roger uses it to pay off the Lender, and then he deeds the property to the Buyer free and clear.

No out-of-pocket, or very little.

And he might even put an Early Payment Penalty clause in the Wraparound Mortgage, and come out with some money.

Roger will definitely make it clear to the Buyer that he is buying the property subject to the underlying financing, which Roger is paying off as he receives payments from the Buyer.

Now, in order to compare this scenario to the outright sale in the prior scenario, let's look at Roger's tax liability at the end of the first year.

The sale of the Duplex with the Wraparound Note will trigger the Capital Gains Tax.

But Roger will only pay the tax at the end of the year in which he receives the income, not all of it up front, like a regular cash-out sale.

And with the Installment Sale, the tax will be paid over 25 years, upon receipt of the monthly payments, which are made up of both interest and principal.

However, only a percentage of the money that is received as a Down Payment, and only a percentage of the Principal portion of each payment will be taxable as Capital Gains, because only a percentage of these payments represents profit.

This percentage is what the IRS calls the "ratio."

Remember, Roger's Basis in the property is $250,000 and he sold it for $375,000, so his Capital Gains is $125,000.

And $125,000 is 1/3 (one-third) of the $375,000 Sales Price.

So, Roger's ratio is 1/3, or 33.33%.

That means that 33.33% of the "principal" portion (not the interest) of each payment that Roger receives, in the year in which he receives it, is considered Capital Gains, and is subject to tax.

This includes the Down Payment that he received in the first year.

Of course, the first $50,000 of the $125,000 of Capital Gains will be treated as Depreciation Recapture and will be taxed up to the rate of 25%, before you even start calculating your Capital Gains.

So, let's look at the first year, and assume that the sale was on January 1.

Roger received $112,500 as a Down Payment.

He received 12 monthly payments of $1,855.30 and the total principal portion of these was $3,670.36.

You can run an Amortization Schedule on $262,500 at 7% for 25 years and verify this.

So, the principal received by Roger in the first year is $112,500 plus $3,670.36, which is a total of $116,170.36.

Multiply this times his ratio of 1/3 and you get $38,723.45.

This is Roger's taxable Capital Gains in the first year.

Since this is less than the $50,000 Depreciation Recapture amount, all of it is taxed at 25%.

Roger's total Capital Gains tax is $9,680.86. That's 25% of $38,723.45.

He pays this from the $375,000 in cash that he is holding and he still has $365,319.14.

That takes care of Roger's after-tax situation from the sale.

Now, let's look at the cash flow from the Note Payments, and the tax consequences of those, if any.

On Roger's Wrap-around Note, he received 12 monthly payments of $1,855.30 for a total of $23,263.60.

On Roger's underlying loan, he made 12 monthly payments of $1,534.55 for a total of $18,414.60.

This gives him a positive annual cash flow of $3,849.

Over the life of the loan this should provide Roger with a total of $96,225.

On the monthly payments that he received, we have already accounted for the tax on the principal portion of those payments for the first year.

His second year tax bill should be 25% of 1/3 of $23,263.60, which is $1,938.63.

His tax bill for the third year, and subsequent years, should be 15% of 1/3 of $23,263.60, which is $1,163.18.

But each payment also contained payment of interest, and this interest payment is also taxable, as "interest income."

The total amount for the twelve payments is $16,737.94.

And, again, I urge you to go to MortgageCalculator.org, and create an Amortization Schedule and print it out.

You should do this every time you are considering a deal. It is the only way you will see the real numbers.

This $16,737.94 is interest income to Roger, and must be reported as such on his tax return, on Schedule B.

But Roger also made payments on his underlying loan, and those payments included both principal and interest.

The principal portion is not deductible, but the total amount of interest that he paid for the twelve payments was $11,928.96.

Is it deductible and if so, where can he deduct it?

Well, it is "mortgage interest," as well as "investment interest."

But it is not deductible as mortgage interest because the debt was not used to buy, build, or improve his personal residence or vacation home.

But Taxpayers can still deduct investment interest as an Itemized Deduction on Schedule A.

And Roger's individual Tax Profile will determine whether he will receive any benefit from doing so.

Roger will continue to report both the principal portion, and the interest portion, of the monthly Note payments that he receives for the duration of the Note.

So, his first year cash position will be $375,000 minus $9,680.86, which is $365,319.

His positive cash flow from the remaining 25 years will be more than enough to cover his annual Capital Gains Tax from the Installment Sale payments, and should provide him with another $83,600.

CONCLUSION

In the first scenario, Roger sells the house outright, and ends up with no property, his $300,000 back and $51,250 in profit.

In the second scenario, Roger still owns the property but has no management responsibilities or monthly expenses, he has $365,320 in cash, he has monthly cash flow of about $280 for 25 years, for about $84,000 in total, his own Mortgage is being paid off with the payments he receives from his Wraparound Note, and he has another $112,500 equity in the property in case he has to take it back.

On his personal Financial Statement, he will list the underlying note as a Liability, and the underlying note payments as Monthly Expenses. But he will also list the Wraparound Note (of an equal amount) as an Asset, and the Wraparound Note Payments as Monthly Income.

If he needed to do so, he could even borrow against the Wraparound Note.

This is what Real Estate Investors call "being in the game." Have as many things going as possible, with the least amount of risk.

It is the reason that some investors never sell property outright.

They find other ways to do it.

SELECTED RESOURCES

AMORTIZATION CALCULATOR

There are a number of online Amortization Calculators, but here is the one that I've used for a long time, and never had a problem.

mortgagecalculator.org

SECTION 1031 SELLER FINANCING

In addition to the Seller Financing scenario that I have discussed here, you might also be interested in doing Seller Financing together with a Section 1031 Like Kind Exchange. It can have great advantages.

So I have included a Chapter from my book "How To Do A Section 1031 Like Kind Exchange."

CHAPTER 13

SELLER FINANCING

Section 1031 of the Internal Revenue Code (IRC) permits you to sell your investment property, called Relinquished Property, and defer taxes on your Capital Gains and Depreciation Recapture, if you purchase another investment property, called your Replacement Property, within 180 days.

SECTION 1031 EXCHANGE RULES

Section 1031 Exchange rules require that the purchase price of your Replacement Property be equal to, or greater than, the sales price of your Relinquished Property.

Section 1031 Exchange rules also require that you use all of your Net Sales Proceeds from the sale of your Relinquished Property in the purchase of your Replacement Property.

SECTION 1031 RELINQUISHED PROPERTY

The question we are dealing with here is whether

you can use Seller Financing in purchasing your Replacement Property.

In other words, can you have the Seller of the Replacement Property finance your purchase from him, instead of you getting a mortgage from a lender?

Let's see how that would work.

Let's use an Example, with simple numbers.

You bought an investment property for $130,000 with a $90,000 mortgage a few years ago.

You have claimed $30,000 in depreciation and you have paid the note down to $80,000.

Now you are selling the property for $300,000.

You have $200,000 in profit, the difference between the selling price and your adjusted basis.

$170,000 of this profit is true Capital Gains, the difference between what you paid for the property ($130,000) and what you sold it for ($300,000).

The other $30,000 of your profit is caused by the claimed depreciation which lowered the Basis in the property.

When you close on the sale, your $300,000 Gross Sales Proceeds will be reduced by the mortgage payoff of $80,000 and you will have Net Sales Proceeds of $220,000.

Now, let's look at the second part of the transaction.

SELLER FINANCED REPLACEMENT PROPERTY

Let's say you purchase a Replacement Property for $410,000.

You must use the $220,000 of Net Sales Proceeds toward the purchase of the property, leaving $190,000 in funding that you must provide.

You can use your own cash for all or part of this amount.

You can get a loan from a lender for the entire $190,000.

You can sign a note back to the Seller for $190,000 and do Seller Financing.

Or you can use any combination of the three.

As long as you buy a Replacement Property of equal or greater value, and you use all of your Net Sales Proceeds in the purchase, it does not matter where or how you finance the rest of the property.

And this includes Seller Financing.

CHAPTER 9

DON'T SIGN THAT DEED-IN-LIEU

OVERVIEW

So you can't make the payments on that Note, it's in Default, and the Lender says, "Instead of me going through the process of Foreclosing, why don't you just sign a Deed In Lieu of Foreclosure back to me, since you're going to lose the property anyway?"

You don't see any downside to this, and you really don't feel that you have any other options, so you agree.

But wait.

There <u>are</u> downsides to doing this, and you need to know what they are.

WHAT HAPPENED

Real Estate has a lifetime, just like people.

But rental real estate is more likely to have a <u>life cycle</u>, or more than one life cycle, as it is periodically rehabbed and updated, and starts a new cycle.

Ten years ago, John bought a small Apartment Building for $500,000.

He assigned $73,750 to the value of the lot and $426,250 to the value of the building, and he put that $426,250 on a Depreciation Schedule, for 27.5 years at $15,500 per year, and has claimed a total of $155,000 in Depreciation so far.

His current Tax Basis in the Apartment Building, the Depreciated Basis, is $345,000.

The property has appreciated in value 7% per year from its original $500,000 and the current FMV is $983,775.

John has refinanced a couple of times over the years, and the recent Mortgage amount was for $775,000.

Shortly after the refinance, a new 200-unit Apartment Complex opened in the area.

It is closer to the main roads, the freeway, the shopping centers, the University, and the restaurants, and is, in general, in a more attractive location.

It has two pools, six tennis courts, and covered parking.

Of course, the rents are higher, and when John heard about it, he expected to lose a few tenants, those who were ready to move up to something like that.

But the new Apartment Complex started offering five months free rent to new tenants who signed an annual lease, and also began marketing aggressively to other apartment residents in the area.

A one-year lease at the new Apartment Complex would actually cost less than a lease at John's Apartment Building.

John lost half of his tenants almost immediately, and when he tried to entice the others into new leases by lowering the rents, they were reluctant, so he was pretty sure that he would be losing them too.

With half of his rental income gone, after a couple of months he could not make his Note payments, except by dipping into his savings.

With the vacancy rate at around 50% and falling, he realized that the market had changed drastically, and he knew that he probably could not sell the property for the amount of the Mortgage, and he did not have the cash to cover the difference in the Mortgage payoff if he sold it for less, assuming that he could sell it at all.

He went to the Lender and told them that he saw no way out, could not continue, and he was willing to work with them to do whatever was necessary.

They suggested that he sign the property over to them, with a Deed In Lieu, which would avoid the necessity of going through a Foreclosure proceeding, which would be a negative experience for both of them.

The Lender really didn't want the property, but they wanted to get possession of the Apartment Building as soon as possible and try to salvage something out of it.

They told John that they would completely relieve him of the debt in return for the Deed In Lieu, and that they would try to convince one of their other customers involved in real estate investing to take the property.

John saw no downside to the arrangement, so without talking to any tax or business experts, he agreed, and the deal was done.

It was tough for John, the Apartment Building had become his whole life, but he tried to adjust and eventually got over it, and was starting to relax.

Then he got the "Notice" from the IRS.

The process is complicated, and walking you through it would be confusing, so I'll just explain the basic concepts.

The IRS looks at the transaction of deeding the property back to the Lender as a sale, with the Sales Price being the FMV of the property at the time of the transaction (not the amount of the forgiven debt).

The FMV of the property was $983,575.

So, in the eyes of the IRS, John had sold the Apartment Building to the Lender for $983,575.

John's Tax Basis in the property was $345,000.

That means that he had a Capital Gains of $638,575.

And that puts him in the 20% Capital Gains Tax bracket.

But before doing that Calculation, he must deal with the portion of his Capital Gains that is attributable to the Depreciation that he has claimed on the property over the ten years that he owned it as rental property.

He has claimed $155,000 in Depreciation, and he must now pay a Depreciation Recapture Tax of 25% on that amount.

His Depreciation Recapture Tax will be $38,750.

On the remaining $483,575 of his regular Capital Gains, he will pay nothing on the first $40,000 because there actually is a 0% Capital Gains Tax bracket, and John qualifies for it because his other income has dropped to zero.

On the next $400,499 he will pay 15%, which will be $60,067.

On the remaining $42,125 he will pay 20%, which will be $8,425.

So, his total Capital Gains Tax will be $68,492.

And the total of his Depreciation Recapture Tax and his Capital Gains Tax together will be $107,242.

This is money that John does not have.

But at least John avoided another potential tax liability, the one for taxation of Cancellation of Debt, called COD income, and we'll discuss that shortly.

If the amount of the debt on the property had been more than the FMV of the property, the difference would have been classified as COD income, and taxed as Ordinary Income.

WHAT SHOULD HAVE HAPPENED

When John decided that he could not continue with the Apartment Building, he researched the situation and realized that if he deeded the property back to the Lender, he could face the consequences of owing a great deal of taxes on phantom income, income that he would not receive but for which he would be liable for the taxes.

And he would not have the income to pay the taxes.

So, instead of deeding the property back to the Lender with a Deed In Lieu Of Foreclosure, he considered the other possibility of a "friendly" Foreclosure in which he cooperated with the Lender to make it go as smoothly as possible.

The Lender would still get the property back just like a Deed in Lieu, and John would still be relieved of the debt.

And the tax consequences would be far less.

John is concerned with two categories of tax liability: Capital Gains and Cancellation of Debt (COD) income; three really, if you consider the two different levels of first one – Depreciation Recapture Tax and regular Capital Gains Taxes.

The amount of his Capital Gains tax liability would be calculated as the difference between his Depreciated Basis, also referred to as Tax Basis, in the property, and the Fair Market Value (FMV) of the property.

The FMV of the property is the major area of concern for John, because the higher it is, the more his tax liability.

And when it come to determining exactly what the FMV is, the IRS will try to find the highest number that they can. And, unfortunately, that would probably be the number in the Appraisal that John had done when he did the last refinance.

But that was over nine months ago, and things have changed significantly, so John has a fair shot at establishing a new FMV that will be more favorable to him.

In his favor is the fact that, although the Lender called the report an "Appraisal" during the loan refinance process, it was actually something that Lenders use called a BPO, a Broker's Price Opinion. This is something done by a Realtor, and can be anything from a simple "drive-by," to a detailed report with "comps."

So, the first thing that John does is get an Appraisal done by a licensed Appraiser, and request that the Appraisal be based on the income-producing value of the property, using his own recent monthly Income Statements, with adjustments then made for changes in the specific market in the last nine months, rather than being based on similar property sales (comps) for the past two years.

The Appraisal came in at $500,000.

John didn't have to use it, but he thought it was probably accurate for the current situation, and he could prove it, so he decided to go with it.

John knew almost all of the people involved in apartment investing in the area, and was friends with a few of them. He found one, Ray, who said he was interested in buying the property at the Foreclosure Auction if the Lender was agreeable to financing 100%, and if John would agree to stay on as Manager.

Together, they went to the Lender and worked out the deal for a friendly Foreclosure, and a verbal agreement regarding Ray purchasing the property at the Auction, in return for the Lender canceling any remaining debt not covered by the proceeds of sale.

John gave the Lender a copy of the Appraisal, because he wanted the Lender to use it.

He knew that the Lender would be providing both him and the IRS with a copy of the Form 1099-A that would report the foreclosure on the property. He also knew that the Form 1099-A, as well as the Form 1099-C that the Lender would file, would contain a box for reporting the "Fair Market Value of the Property."

The Instructions for filing out the Forms say that the FMV is "generally the gross Foreclosure bid price," and this is probably correct when there is not a more accurate and recent determination of the FMV.

But, in all other cases that I am aware of, the IRS will flatly deny that a Foreclosure Sale establishes a FMV, because, they say, it is a "distress sale" and not a normal arms-length transaction that occurred in "the normal course of business."

So, I would be comfortable using the Appraisal number.

The Instructions say "generally," and when the IRS means "always," they say "always," not "generally."

The agreement was reached and the Lender proceeded with the Foreclosure.

Ray bid until the price reached $700,000 and all of the other bidders dropped out.

So the property was sold to Ray for $700,000 and the Lender financed the entire amount, which it then received back as a partial payoff of the outstanding debt, so no money actually changed hands.

The Lender reported to the IRS that it had foreclosed on the property belonging to John, that the Sales Price had been $700,000 and that the remaining $75,000 of the outstanding debt had been canceled.

Then John added up all of his numbers.

His Capital Gains was the difference between the FMV of the property at the time of the Foreclosure and his Depreciated Basis in the property. This was $500,000 less $345,000.

So his Capital Gains came to $155,000.

As with any Capital Gains calculation, the IRS requires that the first tax applied must be the higher of the two taxes involved, since Capital Gains calculations are a mixture of two elements –

Depreciation Recapture and regular Capital Gains.

Depreciation Recapture tax is 25%, and Capital Gains tax is 0-20%, depending on the Taxpayers tax bracket on other income.

John had claimed $155,000 of Depreciation over the ten-year period, so the entire Capital Gains figure of $155,000 was taxed as Depreciation Recapture at 25%.

John was not able to take advantage of the 0% Capital Gains tax bracket.

So, his Capital Gains tax amount was $38,750.

Now, John had to look at whether he was also liable for Cancellation of Debt (COD) Income.

His debt on the property was $775,000 and the property sold at Auction for $700,000 and that amount was applied to his debt, leaving COD Income of $75,000 which the Lender reported to the IRS.

John had researched this matter and knew that there were three ways that he could deal with this additional phantom income so that he would not have to pay taxes on it, since it was taxed at Ordinary Income levels.

The first way to deal with it was to declare Bankruptcy. It was a drastic step and one that he did not want to take.

The second way was to claim that he was "insolvent," meaning that the total of his liabilities was more than the total value of his assets. The IRS would wipe out the obligation if he was, but the process of applying for the determination, and satisfying all of the requirements was drawn-out and burdensome.

The third way was to take other depreciable real estate investment property that he owned, and reduce the Basis in that property by an amount equal to the COD Income. That way, the liability would come up again when the chosen property is sold, but this third alternative had two distinct advantages.

The first advantage is that if the sale of the chosen real estate does happen, and the taxes are paid on the deferred amount, it will be into the future when the dollar is worth less, and it will be at Capital Gains tax rates rather than at Ordinary Income tax rates like COD Income.

The second advantage is that a Section 1031 Like Kind Exchange can be used when the chosen property is sold, and the the Replacement Property can be something like a Triple Net Lease property where he can retire and just sit at home and receive checks. This is what John had been planning to do with the chosen property anyway, so that tax liability just disappeared.

So, John's total tax liability came to $38,750 and he worked out a Payout Arrangement with the IRS for periodic payments, so that he wasn't hit with it all at once.

CONCLUSION

Foreclosure can be a very traumatic situation just from a personal standpoint.

From a business standpoint, it can be a disaster when you are hit with all of the tax liability on income which you will not receive.

It is critical that you plan for the event when you see that it is likely to occur.

Of course, in real world situations, you will probably find that the Lender does not even want to foreclose on the property.

Lenders are not in the business of managing investment real estate, they are not set up to do it. And they realize that you are probably the person best equipped to manage the property. You know more about it than anyone else possibly could.

So, in most cases, the Lender will be willing to restructure your financing so that you can keep the property and try to turn it around.

But if you see that Foreclosure in inevitable, you should definitely sit down with an expert and map out a plan so that those tax numbers will be as low as possible.

SELECTED RESOURCES

PUBLICATION 4681, CANCELED DEBTS, FORECLOSURES, REPOSSESSIONS, AND ABANDONMENTS

This is one of the best Publications from the IRS.

It will answer every question that you could possibly have, and probably provide you with more questions and considerations. You can find it at:

https://www.irs.gov/publications/p4681#en_US_2015_publink1000192059

FORM 1099-A

Form 1099-A, Acquisition or Abandonment of Secured Property ("Abandonment" does not mean just walking away, it means Foreclosure or deeding back to the lien-holder) is the control form that must be filed with the IRS in every situation where there is a Foreclosure, or the recording of a Deed in Lieu.

Here is the site where you can find the IRS position on the tax law, a copy of the Form 1099-A, and a copy of the Instructions which explain what everything on the Form means.

https://www.irs.gov/site-index-search?search=form+1099-a&field_pup_historical_1=1&field_pup_historical=1

FORM 1099-C, CANCELLATION OF DEBT

Form 1099-C, Cancellation of Debt, is the control form that must be filed with the IRS in every situation where there is a Foreclosure, or the recording of a Deed in Lieu, that results in an adjustment of the debt obligation of the borrower.

Here is the site where you can find the IRS position on the tax law, a copy of the Form 1099-C, and a copy of the Instructions which explain what everything on the Form means.

https://www.irs.gov/site-index-search?search=form+1099-c&field_pup_historical_1=1&field_pup_historical=1

FORM 982, REDUCTION OF TAX ATTRIBUTES DUE TO DISCHARGE OF INDEBTEDNESS

If you want to explore the possibility of eliminating the COD Income tax liability by qualifying for the status of "insolvent," then the following link contains an explanation of the law, Form 982, and the Instructions.

https://www.irs.gov/site-index-search?search=form+982&field_pup_historical_1=1&field_pup_historical=1

CHAPTER 10

BUY ME OUT, OR I'LL BUY YOU OUT

OVERVIEW

When (if?) you go into business with someone, the most important consideration is <u>not</u> whether you like that person.

That's a bonus. And a big one.

But before that, you need to consider whether the individual interest of each of you are compatible, and then "align your interests."

Ask yourself the questions.

What do you bring to the table, and what does the other person bring to the table?

What do you expect to receive from the operation, and what does the other person expect to receive?

After you have worked all that out, now comes the important matter of structuring the Agreement between the two of you so that when (if?) you have a disagreement, there is a process for dealing with it.

The process should be, first, a way to resolve the disagreement, and get everything back on track the way you want it.

But secondarily, the process should provide for a manner of undoing everything that has happened so that each of you is "put back into the position you were originally in," or one of you is put back into that position, and the other one carries on the business.

The Agreement that I mentioned will be an "Operating Agreement" in the case of an LLC, and it will be a "Partnership Agreement" in the case of a General Partnership or Limited Partnership.

We won't discuss those Agreements here, there isn't enough time, but we will discuss the way in which you can deal with a disagreement that cannot be dealt with under the terms of the Operating Agreement or Partnership Agreement.

It is called a Buy-Sell Agreement.

You could try to put this into the Operating Agreement or the Partnership Agreement, but my experience is that it is better to have it as a completely separate document, which stands on its own.

You will see why, as we learn about Martha and Larry.

WHAT HAPPENED

Martha and Larry were good friends, and they often had lunch together.

One day, Larry, who was a Salesman at the local Chevy dealership, said, "I had an interesting conversation today with a customer. You know about real estate investments, right?"

Martha, who ran a Bookkeeping Service along with a friend, had mentioned real estate in conversations before.

"Yes," she said. "A number of our clients have real estate investments. I've thought about getting into it myself."

"That's what I thought. You and I never discussed it, but my customer told me something that made me think. He just came back home from College, and his parents have this old Duplex that they really can't manage anymore, and they assumed that he would be taking it over."

"Good for him," Martha said. "Those can be good investments."

Larry said, "Well, that's just the thing. He doesn't want to do it. He has no interest. He came in to talk to me about buying a car, but he thought that since I am a salesman, that I might be interested in selling the Duplex for him. He doesn't trust Realtors, he's had some bad experiences with them."

"Haven't we all," Martha said. "Yeah, I've done the books on a lot of rental properties. So, what do you want to know?"

"Well, actually, I'm thinking about buying the Duplex. But I'm terrible with business and numbers. I wondered if you'd be interested in going in with me. I can do the maintenance. I've worked construction."

It was the beginning of the end of a friendship.

Martha and Larry went on the internet and got a basic LLC package, with a standard Operating Agreement, and set up Endeavor, LLC.

Larry talked to his customer's parents and negotiated a price of $160,000 for the Duplex, each unit a 2-bedroom, 2-bath, and they got Owner Financing, at 5% for 25 years, with no Down Payment, because the parents preferred to have money coming in every month instead of all at once.

And Endeavor, LLC agreed to pay all of the Closing costs.

Martha and Larry set about fixing the place up, and notified the tenants, who were month-to-month, that there would be periodic increases in rent to bring them up to the market average of $1,200.

It was a little rocky at first, but within a year, they had two new tenants, and everything was going well. The Duplex was cash-flowing over $1,000 per month, and all of the deferred maintenance had been done.

Martha and Larry had created a real estate investment that was worth about $200,000 fair market value in that area.

But Martha was always thinking like a businessperson, and one day she said to Larry, "Let me tell you what I've been thinking. I've been talking to my clients about Duplexes. Some of them own them, some don't."

"Yeah?," Larry said.

"They all say that we are lucky, because 2-bedroom, 2-bath units don't usually have a high demand, or a very good future."

"But we are leased up."

"That's why they say we are lucky. There's a shortage of units right now, and we probably have tenants who could not find a 3-bedroom, 2-bath, or couldn't afford one because prices are inflated. They say that nobody is building the smaller units anymore."

Larry said, "Is that true?"

"Well," Martha replied, "I've done some research, and yeah, it mostly is. The 3-2 Duplex is selling for about $320,000 and the units are renting for about $1,600 – $1,800 per month. In those units, the bedrooms and one of the baths are smaller than ours, but the living rooms and kitchen are a little larger."

"But," Larry said, "$1,600 is not that much more than what we're getting."

"Yes, but based on the comps in this area, a 2-2 Duplex should be valued at about $180,000. And based on the 1% rule that real estate investors use, our units should rent for about $900 instead of the $1,200 that we are getting. We just lucked into a tight market. Of course, I think we have nicer construction and a nicer neighborhood. But, still."

"Well, I'm comfortable with where we are. What do you think?"

Martha said, "Well, I've been running the numbers..."

"Of course, you have."

"... and the numbers actually look pretty good," said Martha. "We could add a third bedroom and third bath for each unit right onto the back of the building downstairs. The back door becomes the door to the new bedroom, and we have a new back door. We could make it a Master Bedroom and the bath would be a Master Bathroom. The two upstairs bedrooms would still each have their own bathrooms. Not only would we match the other

3-2s on the market, but we would "outmatch" them. We would have two units that are 3-3 with a Master Bedroom and a Master Bath. We could outclass the market."

"That sounds expensive," Larry said.

"It isn't," said Martha. "It would be a single add-on, one slanted roof, three walls. The plumbing in the kitchens are already on the back wall, so we just come off that. The duct work is in the ceiling, we tie into that. With the slant of the new roof addition, we might lose the back window on the back bedrooms upstairs, but we'll have to see about that. And add-on construction like this is costing about $70 per square foot. Add the bathroom fixtures and another small A/C unit, or we could even go with window units, and the total would be about $40,000."

"I don't know," Larry said. "Everything seems to be going so well."

"And if we wait until it is not going well, which is a real possibility, it will be too late. Look, Larry, we are into this investment now for what, about $6,800 plus Closing Costs, and I was able to claim most of what we paid out as repairs and deduct it from income. We can make this work, and have a property worth at least $320,000. And being a 3-3 and having the Master Bedroom and Master Bath, I'm thinking it would appraise closer to $340,000."

"Look," Larry said, "I'm not a business person, or really even a real estate investor. I'm a car salesman. I love cars and I love selling cars. This is starting to sound like big business to me. Even if it looks better on paper, I'm not sure that it would feel better to me. I think it would feel worse. I like that monthly rental income, and I like not having to spend much time with the property."

Martha and Larry continued to discuss the possibility of upgrading the property.

For Martha, it was obviously a great opportunity, investing $40,000 and increasing market value $120,000. Not to mention increasing monthly cash flow another $400-500 and having a couple of premier units that would always be in high demand for quite some time into the future.

But Larry was happy. The current situation was great, and changing it would mean changing other things in his life, and he was not willing to do that.

When Martha offered to buy Larry's interest in the property, he was offended, and reminded her that he was the one who found the property in the first place.

They just stopped talking about it, but it was always there, and their friendship suffered. They saw less and less of each other, and finally almost stopped talking at all.

Later, when Martha saw more units coming onto the market, some of the new 3-2s available for what they were charging for their 2-2s, she offered to sell her interest to Larry. His response was that he was not interested in taking over the business side of things, and he expected her to stick to her commitment.

With the opportunity to get ahead of the market now gone, they just waited until they would have to start lowering rents, and maybe start having trouble finding tenants at all.

WHAT SHOULD HAVE HAPPENED

Martha and Larry found a great opportunity with the Duplex.

And they were right to take advantage of it.

But they should have discussed it more.

They should have gone to a good Real Estate Attorney who also handles Business Law and Tax Law matters, and asked him how the relationship should be created, and what documents they should have.

He would have asked the right questions, and helped them understand that while they had a very good basis for a <u>friendship</u>, a <u>business relationship</u> is a whole other matter, and needs to be looked at differently.

And just so you will know, in case you ever do this, the first thing that the Attorney will tell you is that he cannot represent you. That's because an Attorney cannot represent two people in the same matter unless they have identical interests, and no two people have identical interests. Therefore, they are considered to have "differing interests" or "conflicting interests" as the law describes it. So the Attorney can't represent both of you at the same time.

Think about it. If he represents you, he is required to draft the Operating Agreement so that you have all of the advantages. That's his job. But what about the other person? The Operating Agreement terms would all be to his disadvantage. And the Attorney is supposed to also be representing the other person, and drafting the operating agreement so that he will have all of the advantages. So he can't do what an Attorney is supposed to do, and still represent both of you.

However, he can represent the LLC. And he will.

Each of you will represent your own interests. In other words, you will represent yourselves, and the Attorney will represent your LLC.

The Attorney will probably set up the LLC Operating Agreement so that each of you have equal control, and equal everything else, unless you tell him to do it differently.

He will also include prescribed methods for dealing with matters in which the two of you find that there is a conflict of interest. And the Agreement will state that if these procedures do not resolve the conflicts, then either party may institute the provisions of the Buy-Sell Agreement, which will state that it "is being executed simultaneously, but as a separate, stand-alone, document."

The Buy-Sell Agreement is made up of two parts.

The first part will establish the circumstances under which an unhappy owner can compel the other owner to either sell his interest to him, or compel the other owner to buy the unhappy owner's interest.

The second part of the Agreement will set out the method of valuation for each owner's interest.

Most of the content that you read concerning a Buy-Sell Agreement will give you a long list of possible circumstances triggering a Buy-Sell event which are vague and go on forever, and probably will not provide you with anything you can mold to fit your circumstances.

The articles and podcasts will also explain a number of formulas for valuing the interests, which will almost always be challenged when the time comes to actually do it.

Therefore, you need to work with the Attorney and craft an Agreement that both of you are comfortable with, and which contains the specific details that both of you will accept when the time comes.

I know that is not very specific, and might not be very helpful.

So let's look at how this will work when Martha and Larry sat down with the LLC Attorney and draft the Buy-Sell Agreement.

The Attorney said, "OK, we are assuming that there will never be a disagreement, and that we will never need this Buy-Sell Agreement. But if we ever do need it, it will save a lot of trouble. So the first thing I need to know is about the property value. What did you pay for it, and what do you both believe that it is worth. In other words, if one of you wanted to sell to the other, and the other wanted to buy, what would that price be?"

Martha said, "Well, we paid $160,000 and with our Closing Costs, and a small amount of fix-up costs, the total was around $170,000. But I think the real market value would be $180,000."

Larry said, "I agree."

"Fine," said the Attorney. "Now, what is the Gross Rental Income, and the Net Rental Income?"

"Well," said Martha. "Right now it is not what it should be. But we intend to raise the Gross Rental Income to $2,400 a month for both units.

And my projected expenses, after we finish a few small deferred maintenance items, will be about $1,700 for both units, so that will leave about $700 total. We'll deduct another $430 Depreciation expense each month, so our cash flow before the principal payment on the note will be about $1,130. And although the principal payment amounts will gradually decrease, it should be about $300 monthly for the first few years, leaving a net of $830 cash flow, which is $415 for each of us."

"So you agree that $700 income, and $830 net cash flow is a reasonable presumption."

"Yes," said Martha, and Larry nodded agreement.

"OK," said the Attorney. "So, could we agree that at any point in the future, the agreed-upon transfer price would be 75 times the Gross Rental Income, like it is now, with 75 times $2,400 equaling $180,000?"

"Well," Larry said, "the value of the property to me is the monthly cash that I get. My other income depends on my car sales, so that $415 is my comfort every month. Could we base it on that? Just asking."

Martha, doing a quick calculation, said, "Sure, we could say that the transfer price would be 216 times the net monthly cash flow, or the average net monthly cash flow for the prior 12 months, just to make it more accurate."

"So it looks like," the Attorney said, "we have nailed down the valuation question. That means that we would take that number, subtract the debt on the property to determine the equity, and divide that by two to determine how much money would actually be paid by the Buyer to the Seller."

"But wait," Martha said, "when the Buyer eventually sells the property, he or she will have to pay the Capital Gains Tax on the profit, and the Depreciation Recapture Tax on the amount of Depreciation claimed. The Seller's accumulated portion of that should be deducted at the time of the transfer."

The Attorney said, "Do you agree, Larry?"

Larry said, "Of course."

"Fine," said the Attorney, "leave that to me to word it in the Agreement. Now we need to decide what will trigger this Buy-Sell Agreement. What will happen or evolve that will require it, other than one party wanting to sell and the other party wanting to buy?"

"Well," said Martha, "if one party wants to sell and the other party does not want to buy, or if both parties decide that they want to sell, I guess we would provide that the property be sold to a third party for the highest price."

"Larry?" the Attorney asked.

"Sure," he said, "but what if one party wants to buy, and the other party does not want to sell, since the property is cash flowing, and still going up in value? That's what I see as a possible problem."

"Well," the Attorney said, "one way I have seen that handled is to figure out what the annual appreciation in value has been for the property, then project that for three years into the future. In other words, make the transfer price what it would be three years later, and pay it now. And you could make the monthly payments match what the Seller is currently receiving in cash flow. That way, the Seller would get three years of bonus appreciation, and continue to receive the monthly payments for a period of time."

"That sounds great," said Martha, "but what if the party still does not want to sell?"

The Attorney said, "Then we put in the 'poison pill,' so to speak. We provide that if the party does not want to sell under those conditions, then the party has to buy the LLC interest under those identical conditions. That will guarantee that if either party wants out, they can get out. Is that what you want?"

Martha and Larry agreed that it would be best to have the Buy-Sell Agreement written that way.

They wanted to continue as friends, enjoying their investment together, but if the unforeseen happened, they wanted to be able to transfer the LLC interest from one to the other in a completely fair manner, and know beforehand what would happen when the time came.

CONCLUSION

Friendships are hard enough to manage and sustain.

When you overlay that with a business relationship, it can become ten times more complex.

To save both your friendship and your business relationship, please give this a lot of thought, and if you decide to go ahead, try to find an Attorney who has been around for awhile and seems to have his own life in order. He's more likely to understand what might happen to you in the future.

Choose one who deals with Real Estate, Taxes, Business Entities, and maybe even Wills and Estate Planning.

Spend time with him, more than one visit would be good, and make sure that he knows what both of you think and feel, and what would be in the best business and personal interest of both of you.

A good Buy Sell Agreement can save a business, it can save a friendship, and it can save your sanity.

CONCLUSION

As I said in the Introduction, Real Estate Investing is not all sunshine and lollipops.

It's a business.

I hope that you now see what I was referring to.

Fortunately, these are not real people that I have told you about. So they did not actually suffer the described consequences.

But real people have made these mistakes, and they have actually suffered the consequences.

Think about what you are doing.

Don't blindly accept the information and advice you find in the real estate forums. Part of it is very good, and helpful, but you don't know which part. And the rest of it can do you real harm.

Good luck, and if there is anything that I can do for you, you can email me at Michael@ MichaelLantrip.com.

And if you have time to leave a Review, I would appreciate it.

Thank you for buying the book.

Made in the USA
Columbia, SC
08 August 2024

40135086R00140